The Hidden Power of the AND-Universe
Abundance, Happiness, Prosperity
– Along Your Spiritual Path

Tom Marcoux
Executive Coach
Spoken Word Strategist
Speaker-Author of 33 books
Blogger, YourBodySoulandProsperity.com

Text and Workbook from

YourBodySoulandProsperity.com

A QuickBreakthrough Publishing Edition

Copyright © 2016 Tom Marcoux Media, LLC
ISBN: 0692647376
ISBN-13: 978-0692647370
2nd Edition, greatly reimagined

All rights reserved. No part of this book may be reproduced or transmitted in any form by any means electronic or mechanical, including photocopying, recording or by any information storage and retrieval system without written permission from the publisher.

QuickBreakthrough Publishing is an imprint of Tom Marcoux Media, LLC. More copies are available from the publisher, Tom Marcoux Media, LLC. Please call (415) 572-6609 or write TomSuperCoach@gmail.com

or visit www.TomSuperCoach.com

or Tom's blog: www.BeHeardandBeTrusted.com

This book was developed and written with care. Names and details were modified to respect privacy.

Disclaimer: The author and publisher acknowledge that each person's situation is unique, and that readers have full responsibility to seek consultations with health, financial, spiritual and legal professionals. The author and publisher make no representations or warranties of any kind, and the author and publisher shall not be liable for any special, consequential or exemplary damages resulting, in whole or in part, from the reader's use of, or reliance upon, this material.:

Other Books by Tom Marcoux:
- Discover Your Enchanted Prosperity
- Emotion-Motion Life Hacks
- Relax Your Way Networking
- Be Heard and Be Trusted: How to Get What You Want
- Nothing Can Stop You This Year!
- Reduce Clutter, Enlarge Your Life
- Darkest Secrets of Persuasion and Seduction Masters
- Darkest Secrets of Charisma
- Darkest Secrets of Negotiation Masters
- Darkest Secrets of Making a Pitch to the Film and Television Industry
- Darkest Secrets of Film Directing

Praise for *The Hidden Power of the AND-Universe* and Tom Marcoux

- "In *The Hidden Power of the AND-Universe*, Tom Marcoux shares the truth about how you can create success and happiness through the Law of Attraction *plus* the Law of Creation and the Law of Being. These insights will help you step up your game and enjoy each day. Get this book!"
– Dr. JoAnn Dahlkoetter, author of *Your Performing Edge* and coach to CEOs and Olympic Gold Medalists

- "You'll be inspired by Tom Marcoux's sincere efforts to help you resolve problems. I recommend his work to anyone in a pickle."
– David Barron, co-author of *Power Persuasion*

Praise for Tom Marcoux's Other Work:

- "Get *Relax Your Way Networking*. Success is built on high trust relationships. Master Coach Tom Marcoux reveals secrets to increase your influence." – Greg S. Reid, author, *Think and Grow Rich Series*

- "In *Reduce Clutter, Enlarge Your Life*, Marcoux will help you get rid of the physical and mental clutter occupying precious space in your life. You'll reclaim wasted energy, lower your stress, and find time for new opportunities." – Laura Stack, author of *Execution IS the Strategy*

- "In *Power Time Management*, Tom Marcoux shares his extraordinary strategies and methods that save you time, make you money and increase your success and happiness. As Tom's client for many years, I have benefited from his wisdom and strategic approach. Do your career and personal life a big favor and get this book." – Dr. JoAnn Dahlkoetter, author of *Your Performing Edge* and to CEOs and Olympic Gold Medalists

- "When you want to get big things done, persuasion skills are crucial. In *Create Your Best Life*, Tom Marcoux shows you how to develop new reflexes and responses so you can become even more influential under stressful situations. As a journalist and publicist, I've observed how some people come across as charismatic and influential, while others fail to get their message across. Tom Marcoux reveals methods that anyone can use to enhance their charisma and influence—and make a big, positive difference in this world ne!" – Danek S. Kaus, author of *You Can Be Famous: Insider Secrets to Getting Free Publicity*

- "In *Be Heard and Be Trusted*, Tom's advice on how to remain true to yourself and establish authentic rapport with clients is both insightful and reality based. He [shows how] to establish oneself as a credible expert."
-Arthur P. Ciaramicoli, Ed.D., Ph.D., author *The Curse of the Capable*

Visit Tom's blog: www.YourBodySoulandProsperity.com

Tom Marcoux

CONTENTS*

Dedication and Acknowledgments I

Book One: Improve Your Life through the AND-Universe, Law of Attraction, Law of Creation and Law of Being 7

Articles are interspersed in this book . . . by guest authors Jeanna Gabellini and Morgana Rae

Use the Power of the "AND-Universe" 18

Law of Creation (3 Steps to Make More Money) . . . More about the Law of Attraction 22

The Law of Attraction and Clearing Subconscious Blocks 30

Raise Your Confidence through the Law of Attraction 57

Handle Anger through the Law of Attraction 63

Book Two: The Law of Attraction - Additional Topics 101

Book Three: The Law of Creation - Additional Topics 117

Book Four: The Law of Being - Additional Topics 125

A Final Word and Springboard to Your Success 137

Special Offer Just for Readers of this Book 137

Excerpt from *Darkest Secrets of Persuasion and Seduction Masters: How to Protect Yourself and Turn the Power to Good* 138

About the Author Tom Marcoux 147

* This page has highlights. Even more material is in this book!

DEDICATION AND ACKNOWLEDGEMENTS

This book is dedicated to the terrific book and film consultant, and author Johanna Ellen Mac Leod. It is also dedicated to the other team members. Thanks to Barry Adamson II (of MyWordsforSale.com) for editing. Thank you to David MacDowell Blue for insights and editing on a section.

Thanks to guest authors Jeanna Gabellini and Morgana Rae. [Their articles remain with their original copyright and are included in this book by their permission.]

Thanks to Johanna Ellen Mac Leod for the front cover and back cover. Thanks to my father, Al Marcoux, for his concern and efforts for me. Thanks to my mother, Sumiyo Marcoux, a kind, generous soul. Thank you to Higher Power. Thanks to our readers, audiences, clients, my graduate/college students and my team members of
Tom Marcoux Media, LLC. The best to you.

BOOK ONE: IMPROVE YOUR LIFE BY ACCESSING THE HIDDEN POWER OF THE AND-UNIVERSE (COMBINE THE LAW OF ATTRACTION, LAW OF CREATION AND LAW OF BEING)

The airplane wing raced toward my cameraman's head. He was supposed to crouch down and let the wing swoosh safely over him. But he was standing. As the feature film director, I watched the whole set—in this case, the runway at San Luis Obispo airport. I ran, grabbed the cameraman, pulled him downward—and the wing cut the air above our heads.

As I caught my breath, I was grateful that I had not hesitated and that I had acted swiftly to protect my crew member. And I was grateful and excited that *I was directing my first feature film.*

Later, upon reflection, I realized that *manifesting* my big, first-time director opportunity was not just the product of the Law of Attraction. Two other Laws were involved: the *Law of Creation* and the *Law of Being*.

With even more reflection, I also realized that the *Hidden Power of the AND-Universe* had worked in my

favor. In a moment, I'll provide "working definitions" of the Three Laws: Law of Attraction, Law of Creation and Law of Being.

First, let's observe: **The combined effect of the Three Laws is creating your life of prosperity, love, joy and fulfillment.** For you to experience these benefits, I serve as your coach in this book.

Before we go further, I'll share some details about the *AND-Universe*.

The Hidden Power of the AND-Universe:

The universe has a myriad of textures and facets. However, many of us have been conditioned in such a way that much of the universe remains hidden. How? Our brains relate easily to the "binary pattern": yes/no; hot/cold; friend/enemy; high/low; spiritual/pragmatic; light/dark and more. *The universe is MORE than that!* We can see that the universe has extraordinary facets. For example, light sometimes functions as if it were a wave and in other situations it seems to function like a particle. Could light be both AND neither?

We see paradoxes in proverbs. One holds: "Look before you leap." And another proverb emphasizes: "He who hesitates is lost." Can the truth in a given moment be either, both or neither of these proverbs?

Here are some brief examples of how we can look at "AND" as an empowering facet of the universe.

- We can be grateful AND go for more (as in more joy and more prosperity).
- We can be happy in the moment AND endure uncertainty.
- We can experience gratitude for what we have AND gratitude for what we no longer have to endure (physical

illness; a former, unhealthy relationship and more).
- We can strive for a better life AND we can take a breath at any point in the day and feel inner peace

We can see "AND" in the Serenity Prayer:
God grant me the serenity to accept the things I cannot change; courage to change the things I can; and wisdom to know the difference. – Reinhold Niebuhr

We can hold a healthy form of humility "AND" celebrate the blessings that are within us:
Our deepest fear is not that we are inadequate. Our deepest fear is that we are powerful beyond measure. It is our light, not our darkness that most frightens us. We ask ourselves, 'Who am I to be brilliant, gorgeous, talented, fabulous?' Actually, who are you not to be? You are a child of God. Your playing small does not serve the world. There is nothing enlightened about shrinking so that other people won't feel insecure around you. We are all meant to shine, as children do. We were born to make manifest the glory of God that is within us. It's not just in some of us; it's in everyone. And as we let our own light shine, we unconsciously give other people permission to do the same. As we are liberated from our own fear, our presence automatically liberates others. – Marianne Williamson

You are allowed to be both a masterpiece and a work in progress, simultaneously. - Sophia Bush

In this book, we'll see how the AND-Universe can help us—as we connect with the Law of Attraction AND the Law of Creation AND the Law of Being.

Now, here are the definitions:

Law of Attraction: The operating principle of the universe that "similar energies are drawn together."

Positive thoughts act like magnets to positive life experiences and negative thoughts (given too much attention) attract negative life experiences.

Law of Creation: The operating principle of the universe that when you take action you create new possibilities. Often you are creating new impressions in other people's thoughts. People start to view you as a "mover and shaker." Their confidence in you and your project increases. Action breeds more action and more attraction of people and resources to make your dreams come true.

Law of Being: The operating principle of the universe that renewal and gratitude nourish you so you can have sustained prosperity, abundance and fulfillment. The central idea of the Law of Being is to shift to an empowered state of being. A reliable way to experience more joy and peace is to focus on what you're grateful for.

* * *

With this section, I want us to hit the ground running. So I'll now provide brief and pertinent information about *the Three Laws*.

First, I invite you to take a "let's take a look" approach to the material.

There are more things in heaven and earth, Horatio,
Than are dreamt of in your philosophy.
- Hamlet (1.5.167-8) by William Shakespeare

When I reflected on the successes that my clients and I

have enjoyed in life, I realized that *the combined effect of the Three Laws* manifests amazing, positive outcomes.

I then taught this to my clients, audiences and students in a quick memorable form: **the 3 A's.**

The 3 A's:
- Attraction
- Action
- Abundance

We can see how the elements correspond:
- Attraction (Law of Attraction)
- Action (Law of Creation)
- Abundance (Law of Being).

Now we'll explore further . . .

Law of Attraction

I'll now focus on two elements of the Law of Attraction:

1) To really invoke the Law of Attraction, go beyond the standard "Ask, Believe, Receive" process.
2) The Law of Attraction involves both spiritual and physical processes.

1) To really invoke the Law of Attraction, go beyond the standard "Ask, Believe, Receive" process.

A truly popular description of the Law of Attraction process is: "Ask, Believe, Receive." You get clear about a personal heartfelt desire; then you ask the universe for that desire. Then you visualize the actual experience of receiving the desired outcome or object. Such visualization involves as many senses as possible. You come to truly *believe* that the desired outcome is yours. And the universe delivers what you want.

I've learned that the Law of Attraction process has many layers and textures.

What really helps is to create *a combined effect* of the three laws: Law of Attraction, Law of Creation and Law of Being.

What's missing from many people's attempt to use the Law of Attraction is *action*. Take action (invoke the Law of Creation) and discover that you become even more attractive to positive outcomes, opportunities and resources.

2) The Law of Attraction involves both spiritual and physical processes.

Numerous people report that their prayers attracted good outcomes. Others suggest that after coming to peace about a situation through meditating, they enjoyed a positive resolution to a conflict-laden situation.

By these examples, it's easy to see a spiritual connection with the Law of Attraction.

The law of attraction is the attractive, magnetic power of the Universe that draws similar energies together. It manifests through the power of creation, everywhere and in multiple ways. . . . This law attracts thoughts, ideas, people, situations and circumstances. The law of attraction manifests through your thoughts, by drawing to you thoughts and ideas of a similar kind, people who think like you, and also corresponding situations and circumstances. It is the law and power that brings together people of similar interests. - Remez Sasson

Further, some people suggest that the Law of Attraction may be describing part of the effect of mirror neurons. Mirror neurons are brain cells in the premotor cortex that respond when we perform an action and also when we see someone else perform that action. (noted at The DNA Learning Center website). Research has demonstrated that when people view altruistic or positive behaviors by other people, the same neurons are stimulated in the observers' brains.

You can note this for yourself. Recall a time that you approached someone in a positive manner and the person responded in kind with positive cooperation. In essence, your brain cells stimulated the other person's brain cells to a good outcome.

Now It's Your Turn

Verify the efficacy of the Law of Attraction. Can you recall a time when you thought of a friend, and he or she immediately called you on the phone? Do you remember holding a positive expectation and then you walked into a situation and people cooperated well? Some people report that they told themselves, "I'm going to impress them during the job interview"—and in turn, the job interview went extremely well!

Law of Creation

Two elements of the Law of Creation are:
1) The Law of Creation *enhances* the Law of Attraction.
2) The Law of Creation functions at its peak when you invoke the spiritual processes of nonjudgment, nonresistance and nonattachment.

1) The Law of Creation *enhances* the Law of Attraction.

Several people have complained bitterly that they have practiced "Ask, Believe, Receive" but no heartfelt, desired outcome manifested.

On the other hand, successful people report that they have taken massive amounts of action. They report that such activity made the real difference.

Why would this be so? When you do something, you are creating new possibilities. When you take positive action, you increase the energy that guides a positive return on your invested time, effort and attention.

2) The Law of Creation functions at its peak when you invoke the spiritual processes of nonjudgment, nonresistance and nonattachment.

In a few pages below, I present three separate sections that explore nonjudgment, nonresistance and nonattachment in the context of how you can bring more money into your life. Here I will share that nonjudgment, nonresistance and nonattachment *dissolve hesitation and procrastination to your taking action.*

Now It's Your Turn

Verify the efficacy of the Law of Creation. Can you recall a time when you took action and then enjoyed a positive outcome? Perhaps, you sent out a resume and landed a job opportunity just in time.

Law of Being
The Law of Being includes two particular elements:
1) Feeling grateful places you into an empowered state of being.
2) Doing your duty without renewal gums up the

system of positive manifesting.

1) Feeling grateful places you into an empowered state of being.

To invoke the Law of Being does not require a weekend away at a spa (although that would be nice!)

It involves consciously changing the direction of your thoughts *to gratitude.*

Remember, if you are criticizing, you are not being grateful. If you are blaming, you are not being grateful. If you are complaining, you are not being grateful. — Rhonda Byrne

A grateful heart supercharges the Law of Attraction and Law of Creation. A grateful heart attracts blessings. If you catch yourself complaining about something in your life, try this method: Quickly say out loud, this phrase (and fill in the blank): "I am grateful for _____."

Here's how it works:

- Oh! They're changing the rules again. They've doubled my work but not my pay. *I am grateful for* steady work.
- Again! My husband left the toilet seat up! *I am grateful that* he really is considerate about 98% of the time. He must be tired.
- Damn! I gained two pounds. *I'm grateful that* I got the new treadmill working and I find it's okay to use when I read and walk simultaneously. Two pounds is better than four. Let's see how I'm doing after four days of 30 minutes on the treadmill daily.

When you focus on gratitude, you have an actual experience of the Abundance already present in your life. (Recall, Abundance is the third part of the 3 A's.)

I've learned that to attract more of what you want, it truly helps to pay attention to blessings you already have. The universe responds positively. For example, if you take good care of your current finances, often the universe will give you more finances to work with.

I believe if you keep your faith, you keep your trust, you keep the right attitude, if you're grateful, you'll see God open up new doors. –Joel Osteen

The Law of Being flows in your life when you make time and turn your attention to what you are grateful for in this present moment.

A grateful heart is a beginning of greatness. It is an expression of humility. It is a foundation for the development of such virtues as prayer, faith, courage, contentment, happiness, love, and well-being. - James E. Faust

I feel grateful because I have a lot of love in my life.
– Gisele Bundchen

2) Doing your duty without renewal gums up the system of positive manifesting.
Making consistent choices to renew your personal energy forms a vital element of the Law of Being.

This became all too clear to me several years ago. My father repeated a summary of his philosophy when he said, "Do your duty."

"I do my duty and it doesn't make me happy," I replied. From that moment forward, I realized that I needed more than action and attraction. I needed to feel calm, peace and gratitude for the abundance already present in my life.

Related to the Law of Being, I learned about the value of "just being" after accomplishing a number of things. Mere accomplishments do not add up to happiness. Accomplishments are just *part* of the journey.

I'm grateful for life. And I live it—I believe life loves the liver of it. I live it. – Maya Angelou

An Important Point about Balancing Duty with Renewal

Talk with a beleaguered single mother, and you'll hear how extremely tough it is to take care of one or more children and work, too.

With so much responsibility, she may forego sleep.

Earlier I said, *making consistent choices to renew your personal energy forms a vital element of the Law of Being.*

Here's a real insight: Renewing your personal energy simply makes things function better.

For example, like other entrepreneurs, I awaken in the morning with my mind full of ideas to implement. I'm excited about what I do and I may be tempted to rise without getting enough sleep. However, I'm aware of the Law of Being. So I keep a log of my sleep hours. In this way, I'm making good choices like going back to bed in the morning to get enough sleep.

The Law of Being calls each of us to consciously and consistently make choices that renew our personal energy and feelings of inner peace and joy.

The Law of Being calls on us to devote time and space to rest, renewal and recovery. When you're in a moment of rest, you can realize that you are experiencing a *moment of abundance*. For example, if you rest in a recliner, you have the abundance of that chair in your home. If you eat a good meal to renew your personal energy, you're enjoying the abundance of that meal.

Get the Law of Attraction and the Law of Creation to truly enhance your life: Take action for renewal so the Law of Being works to empower you.

Now It's Your Turn

Verify the efficacy of the Law of Being. Can you recall a time when you got more sleep, felt better and your next day flowed smoothly? Do you agree that renewing your personal energy increases you ability to perform and even attract positive responses in other people?

Create New Opportunities for You – Use the Power of the "AND-universe"

"I really want to increase my income, but I feel like something is holding me back. Something inside me," my friend Sean said.

"Let me share with you the idea of *'This is an AND-universe.'* In this case, I'm talking about how you can be full of gratitude AND 'go for more,'" I replied.

When I speak on *Discover Your Enchanted Prosperity*, I often work with people who are stuck because they were shut down by limiting beliefs in childhood. They heard comments like "just be grateful for what you have and don't be greedy."

Such a concept can function as **chains** on one's energy, viewpoint and fulfillment of personal potential. How? Many of us do not want to be "bad" or "greedy." That's understandable. Still, **I know people who have devoted themselves to serving customers** *and* **they have earned a terrific, prosperous way of life.** Did you see the powerful word? It's **"AND."**

Many of us notice that there is a "gap" between where we are now and where we want to be. But it is folly to say, "I'll only be happy when XY happens." **So the better plan is to enjoy this moment AND "go for more."** You'll find that you can even *enjoy* the process of finding out how you can serve more people in different ways.

We'll use the G.A.P. process:

G – gratitude

A – action

P – preparation

1. Gratitude

Gratitude is a strong stance. When I was trained in karate moves, the instructors guided me to have a strong stance. Such a stance provided support so one could kick. Still, such a stance was *flexible* so you could move in any direction

Gratitude fills us with positive energy. We can shift to gratitude and step out of a mood of disappointment or even a mood of worry.

To begin the shift, write on a sheet of paper (or in a personal journal), **"I am grateful for..."** Now note 10 things that you appreciate in your life.

Many years ago, I worked as part of tech-group inside a top bank. This position did *not* employ my best talents. Still, every morning, I recited my *10 Blessings* as I took a shower.

I'd say, "I'm grateful for my sweetheart, my excellent health, my friends, the financial abundance of my job ..."

This practice helped me enjoy my present moment AND energized me to even work on my own company after returning from the bank each day.

Numerous authors have noted the value of starting from gratitude. **The universe sends more opportunities to you — and you have MORE to be grateful for.**

2. Action

One of my favorite quotes is:

"Replace worry with action." – Steve Chandler

Have you noticed that worried people get stuck? And some miserable people truly spread misery! Instead, we have two ways to develop more and better in our lives.

1) Shift to an outlook of gratitude

2) Take action.

"Actions seems to follow feeling, but really actions and feeling go together; and by regulating the action, which is under the more direct control of the will, we can indirectly regulate the feeling."

– William James

I've noted that when I implement "Replace worry with action," **I simply feel better.**

All I need to do is a simple action. It can be just listing the next people for me to call. I make a couple of phone calls and I feel much better.

Now it's your turn. What small simple actions can you take to get yourself moving in a positive direction?

3. Preparation

I have coached thousands of people (clients and audiences) with this phrase: "Courage is easier when I'm prepared."

By this I mean, that my preparation quiets down my fear and I take action to improve my circumstances.

I'll add this phrase:

The Answer to Fear is Rehearsal.

In college, I had to direct a final project: a live television show. I was afraid. I went to a senior and asked for advice. Paul said, "Don't bury your head in your script. Watch your monitors."

So I went back to my dorm room and drew five "TV Monitors" on five separate sheets of paper. I taped them to the wall. I rehearsed by glancing at the script and then up at the monitors.

When I directed that live television show, I was glad I had rehearsed.

While Camera One was "live"—the background painting visible on Camera Two fell down.

Calmly, I had the crew fix the background during a commercial break.

Rehearsal had saved the day [at least the project and my grade].

Recently, I was invited to give a brief speech. Two weeks later, I stepped on stage and I did well. I know that my 15 rehearsal sessions helped! (Yes, I keep a *Progress Log* of my rehearsals. ... By the way, you can rehearse a section during a phone call with a friend. I often rehearse in a car while a team member drives.)

Now it's your turn. What form of preparation or rehearsal can help you do better when you're in a pressure-filled moment? How will you schedule some rehearsal?

As an Executive Coach, I help new business owners and seasoned professionals free themselves from the chains of limited thinking and lack of consistent action.

When I talk about *Discover Your Enchanted Prosperity*, I

inspire the audience to realize that this is an "AND-universe." **You can enjoy the moment as you focus on gratitude AND you can "go for more."**

How will you approach each day with BOTH gratitude and taking action to create new and better in your life?

We'll now turn our focus on the Law of Creation and the three steps to increase income.

LAW OF CREATION
(3 STEPS)

Law of Creation—Make More Money (Step 1: Nonjudgment)

Have you ever had an idea but immediately thought "That won't work" or "I don't have the skills or education to make that happen"?

Those were instant judgments that likely shut you down.

Worse yet, those may simply have been "voices from your past," perhaps, from a parent or guardian that do NOT apply to you now!

A big problem human beings face is a tendency to instantly judge things. If you think about it, our ancestors survived because they instantly judged things—like "That animal may kill me so I'll climb this tree!"

Those kind of instant judgments help on the savanna, or if you're in a crosswalk and have to dodge an errant car. But such automatic judgments can paralyze a person on the path to creating wealth.

The truth is: To create wealth you need to do new things. You cannot let instant judgments dissolve your resolve to take action.

In various sections of this book, I emphasize **The Power of Your Second Thought.**

Your first thought may be a judgmental thought that is tied with fear. Your Power manifests in your Second Thought.

It's crucial to condition ourselves to have an *Empowering Second Thought.*

Let's say you have a thought for a new product.

Instant Judgmental Thought: That won't work.

Empowered Second Thought: **What if it could work?** What knowledge, resources or new action may be involved?

The people who get "average results" or "normal results" allow themselves to react to new ideas with *instant judgments*—and only instant judgments.

However, the successful people I've interviewed demonstrated that they could hold a vision and look for ways to make something work.

Here are some Empowered Second Thoughts:
- How can I learn something new to make this work?
- Who can help me?
- Is my heart being called into the new venture?
- Am I just fearful? Or perhaps, I'm a bit excited about new possibilities.

To make more money, many of us will really unleash both the Law of Creation and the Law of Attraction by *practicing nonjudgment.* Instead of staying stuck in instant judgmental thoughts, we stay flexible and ask questions and open the door for further possibilities.

You never suffer from a money problem, you always suffer from an idea problem. – Robert H. Schuller

Now that notion might seem extreme. But Pastor Robert Schuller actually applied the concept of "idea problem" when he wanted to raise millions of dollars to make a Crystal Cathedral.

He gave himself access to a lot of ideas.

To raise $10 million, he wrote:

Find:

1,000 people to donate $1000.

100 people to donate $10,000.

10 people to donate $1 million.

He also asked a prosperous friend about how to raise money. His friend said, "If you were going to hunt moose, you would go where the moose are."

So Robert Schuller took these ideas and found where prosperous people were and began raising the funds. From 1981 to 2010, the Crystal Cathedral served millions who visited (and saw the related, weekly television program "Hour of Power").

I've attended service at the Crystal Cathedral. It's amazing.

And in 2016, after renovations, it will reopen and serve many more.

Get the Law of Creation flowing in your life. Seek to be nonjudgmental. Be flexible and grow into the next, great chapter of your life.

Principle
Move beyond instant judgmental thoughts. Stay flexible and ask good questions.

Power Questions
How can you stay conscious of your judgmental thoughts? How will you stay flexible and find new resources and new ideas?

Law of Creation—Make More Money (Step 2: Nonresistance)

Would you like prosperity to flow into your life with a minimum of effort and difficulty?

The spiritual practice of *nonresistance* plus the Law of Creation maximizes abundance on many occasions.

For example, when I come up with a book project, I go with my intuition and get right to work. However, there are times when the marketplace will surprise me.

For example, I wrote a book that is another part of my series *Darkest Secrets of . . . How to Protect Yourself.* The title of this book was *Darkest Secrets of Business Communication.* It discussed ways to help the reader avoid mistakes that often create needless confusion and trouble in the business arena.

However, I was greatly surprised when the book didn't sell many copies. My previous titles including *Darkest Secrets of Persuasion and Seduction Masters* and *Darkest*

Secrets of Film Directing had sold copies every month.

I decided to practice *nonresistance*. I came up with a way to greatly revise the material and release it as a 2nd edition entitled: *Secrets of Awesome Dinner Guests: What Walt Disney, Steve Jobs, Oprah Winfrey, Albert Einstein, Martin Luther King, Jr., Helen Keller and John Lasseter Can Teach You About Success and Fulfillment*. Now, the book sells well.

Nonresistance has a *great benefit* to bestow upon you: you avoid needless emotional upset and loss of time.

Here's the big difference. People who get "average results" or "normal results" often resist what the world or reality is telling them.

When my book wasn't selling, the marketplace was telling me: "You're not serving us in the way we want to be served."

I did not waste a moment trying to "educate people." Instead, I found another way that was "enticing to people."

In fact, I relaxed and did a few other things. I did a video that I posted on YouTube entitled "Use Walt Disney's Strategy for Success . . . with Tom Marcoux." The good responses that people posted to me on Facebook inspired me to expand the idea to "Secrets of Awesome Dinner Guests: What Walt Disney . . ." as you saw above.

Practice nonresistance and let the ideas flow.

Principle

Approach a problem in the spirit of flowing and adapting.

Power Questions

How can you adapt to a situation? Can you revise your

approach? Can you ask people for ideas about what's really important to them? How can you serve people in the way they prefer to be served?

Law of Creation — Make More Money (Step 3: Nonattachment)

Have you found yourself ruminating about something that is just not going your way? Nonattachment provides a graceful way for you to feel better and even get more done.

The essence of nonattachment is to turn "demands" into "preferences."

For example, if Shirley insists that the only good result is for her first book to be a bestseller, then she may face huge disappointment. The result of "bestseller" is only *one* of many positive results.

Bestselling author Richard Carlson told me that his top-selling book *Don't Sweat the Small Stuff* was his 10th book. He loved to write and he pressed on through nine books before he had his first bestselling book.

Nonattachment can seem foreign to many people. Certainly we do feel attached to our friends and family. However, we can enjoy better relationships with them if we do NOT insist that they act, always in the way we think best.

As a comparative religion instructor guiding college students for over 14 years, I have explained,

"Nonattachment is having preferences and NOT demands."

When you walk into situations without a demand, you can "be in this present moment."

One does not stay in the past with regrets or anger about a family member's unkind remarks, for example. And one does not "go into the future"—worrying about poor treatment.

For example, my father is in his late 70s and his comments (as he gets older) have been mean to family members. He is an upset, unhappy, old guy.

When I travel to visit my father and mother, I have no idea what will happen, that is, whether my father will be mean or neutral with his words.

I seek to "walk into the moment fresh." Here's one reason: To walk into the moment already upset over past bad behavior by my father does *not* help.

A number of spiritual paths urge people to not attach themselves to an idea of how they want someone else to be. People only change when they want to.

Otherwise, the person who demands another person be different creates his or her *own* internal suffering.

Before we go further, it would help for me to clarify that there can be "non-negotiables"—particularly in romantic relationships. For example, one of my clients told her boyfriend, "No illegal drugs in my home. I am a school teacher." It's perfectly understandable that she wants to guard her reputation and that she is attached to her job teaching grammar school kids. That's a straight forward non-negotiable detail.

However, if we hold to the idea of nonattachment, we can actually feel inner peace and enjoy the moments as they arrive.

Here's how we can be non-attached when we're looking to create more prosperity.

Gently ask questions like:
- Will this serve many people?
- Does this have a good chance to make profit?
- Will we learn something by doing it?

Some projects are "the projects that train us to do better next time."

For example, actress and singer Cher, starred in the 1969 feature film *Chastity*. The film flopped badly, and it's reported that Cher avoided acting for more than a decade due to the debacle.

Anyone who saw *Chastity* would *not* imagine that Cher would win the Best Actress Academy Award in 1988 for *Moonstruck*.

Good for Cher! She took courageous steps forward.

At some point, *many people find it necessary to shake off the dust of defeat and move forward.*

Nonattachment comes in when we focus on doing our best *in this moment.*

You learn that the fulfilling part is the doing.

– Ed Harris (nominated for 4 Academy Awards)

Ed refers to acting, and he mentioned that one of his own favorite performances is in the feature film *Copying Beethoven*. He was pained that the distributor did not promote the film on release.

So Ed's full comment is: "You learn that the fulfilling part is the doing. I don't count on anything else."

My point about nonattachment is that as you stay flexible you'll be able to leap at new opportunities that will surprise you. It's said that comedian Jimmy Durante began more as a musician. But he saw how people related to his big nose and jokes and threw himself into comedy.

Such a move led to his stardom.

Truly, when you want to create more prosperity in your life, use the wisdom and the peace of nonattachment.

Principle
Free up your possibilities. Move beyond staying attached to first judgments or even disappointments. Be flexible.

Power Questions
How can you reframe your perception on some disappointments? Could they be a springboard to your next chapter of life?

Law of Attraction and Clearing the Blocks

A number of people report that they attempt to use the classic three steps of the Law of Attraction: Ask, Believe, Receive but they do *not* get the results they crave.

What's going on here? Some of us have strong, subconscious blocks that interfere with the Law of Attraction fully working in our lives.

Here are examples of Blocks:
A person . . .
- feels twisted about money
- feels unworthy of success
- feels his or her success "takes away" from someone else

- feels afraid of losses that may come with success
- does not feel a Deep Need to do what's necessary to succeed

To get the Law of Attraction working well, turn these around:

A person
- feels clean and comfortable about money
- feels worthy and happy about success
- feels his or her personal success serves other people
- feels strong and able to withstand the losses that may come with success—and feels sure that the losses "make space" for better people, things and opportunities to now fit into one's life
- feels (everyday) a Deep Need to do what's necessary to succeed

Clear the Blocks

Before we get started with clearing the blocks that occur when applying the Law of Attraction, realize that these blocks begin on the subconscious level. So I'm including sections labeled "Working on the Subconscious Level" in the material below.

1. Clear a feeling of "twisted about money"

Years ago, I had a roommate who was comfortable about money. If he saw that the household box was low on funds, he'd simply go to the roommates and say, "Oh, the household box is a bit low. We're saving to paint the kitchen. Would you get in your monthly contribution before Thursday?"

This roommate even ran a church in which he posted the

church's full budget of income and expenditures in the newsletter. My roommate was "clean and comfortable about money." You could even see his exact salary, which was low.

He did not let himself sit in embarrassment about his low salary.

I'm *not* inviting you to reveal your salary to other people. However, I am inviting you to "reveal your money situation to *yourself*." By this I mean, ask yourself, "Do I have limiting beliefs about money that are holding me back?"

A number of authors point out that limiting beliefs can *restrict* our actions. A limiting belief is recognized by how it stops you from entertaining the possibility of making a true, positive change. It might be characterized by the whining phrase: "It will never work." Limiting beliefs prevent us from making empowering choices.

Worse yet, if you act in a self-sabotaging manner you could be shutting down the efficacy of the Law of Attraction in your life! Further, failing to act can also be self-sabotage.

The following limiting beliefs contribute to what I call "twisted about money."

- Money is the root of all evil. [The actual Biblical quote is: "The *love* of money is the root of all evil."]
- You have to give up too much to be wealthy.
- "Behind every great fortune lies a great crime." – Honore de Balzac

That last comment about "great crime" is one that my father has repeated many times, and I witnessed how he could *not* bring himself to save any money. This limiting belief also *prevented* my father from looking at multiple ways to earn money.

To stop my father's "great crime" comment from being a virus to hurt me, I immediately remind myself of the *benevolent prosperity* author Richard Carlson earned. I've coined the term "benevolent prosperity" to refer to a fortune built on truly serving others. Richard served others as author and speaker. He was best known for writing the *Don't Sweat the Small Stuff* series of books. I know he earned $20,000 a speech (a high fee several years ago) because one of my colleagues called to hire him for her conference.

When Richard Carlson and I were both guest experts on a radio show, he went out of his way to share with me tips for enhancing my work as a speaker and author. What a good and kind mentor!

Richard Carlson is one of the shining examples that *you can add good work to the world and the world provides abundance right back.*

Here's a phrase I tell myself: *Money is a tool I handle well for my good and all involved.*

When I affirm that phrase, I repeatedly remind myself that my earning money ultimately serves all involved. It is a good thing.

Working on the Subconscious Level

I've learned that impacting the subconscious mind takes multiple approaches.

One powerful approach is to *consciously monitor your stories:* stories you tell others, stories you watch and listen to, and *stories you tell yourself.*

Stories are what stick with you.

So our first method is: **Replace the Stuck Story**. I describe the Stuck Story as any tale that holds you back.

Consider telling yourself stories that involve positive outcomes. Make it a conscious choice. It can be a simple story of "I found $5.00 on the bus. I'm lucky."

Also tell stories about how other people performed good deeds, earned opportunities and became prosperous.

2. Clear the feeling of "unworthy of success"

Years ago, I was in Hollywood, running an audition. As both writer and feature film director, I was looking for a rising actor to play the lead ("Alan") of a screenplay I wrote titled, *TimePulse**. I also put out the word that we were looking for the two women leads as well.

I had five people sort through 807 submitted headshots (photos of actors). I saw 21 people in one day.

The big test (although the actors auditioning for "Alan" did not know it) was how the actors would say a particular line.

"Sir Gawain was being tested to see if he was worthy or not."

I was hoping to see the actors study the pages and find the hidden key to the scene. When Alan tells the story and says "worthy or not" he's talking about *himself*.

That day, no actor found a way to communicate the line in a way that showed me he had *become* the lead character. The character Alan is a guy who talks about stories of "feeling unworthy." He *does not* feel worthy.

Feeling worthy or not is *big deal* when it comes to the Law of Attraction and receiving the abundance of the universe.

If you practice telling the story that you are not worthy enough or good enough, *the universe will take you at your word*. This can be terrible. It even becomes a self-fulfilling prophesy. A person can accumulate experiences in which something good was about to happen but then "things fell apart." If someone adds, "Oh, I wasn't ready, anyway," it can add more injury. It can block off the Law of Attraction in helping you through life.

* TimePulse *became a book:* TimePulse Beyond: Titanic *available at Amazon.com*

What's the answer?: **Stop telling those "unworthy me" stories! I mean it.**

There are some confusing details that trip many people up. We see confusion among these words: Proud, Stuck up, Conceited, Self-Esteem, Arrogant, Self-centered.

Self-esteem is NOT connected to the other words. Here is a valuable definition:

"Self-esteem is the disposition to experience oneself as being competent to cope with the basic challenges of life and of being worthy of happiness. It is confidence in the efficacy of our mind, in our ability to think. By extension, it is confidence in our ability to learn, make appropriate choices and decisions, and respond effectively to change. It is also the experience that success, achievement, fulfillment — happiness — are right and natural for us. The survival-value of such confidence is obvious; so is the danger when it is missing." – Nathaniel Branden

In a nutshell, self-esteem is *not* about self-centeredness. Instead, self-esteem is about having the capacity to cope with challenges in life and the ability to thrive!

Further, not having self-esteem, or feeling unworthy, can create a terrible block to a good flow of the Law of Attraction.

There is a controversy about the ways to raise self-esteem. A number of people report that using affirmations like "I feel terrific" actually make them feel worse. They report, "I do not like lying to myself. It feels even worse."

So now, we'll turn our attention to a powerful idea:

It's easier to act your way into a new way of thinking, than think your way into a new way of acting. – Jerry Sternin*

[* There are numerous people who reference this idea. It's not clear who said it first.]

So instead of just repeating certain phrases, I invite you to *take action*. Below, I share the method: ***Prove It to Yourself.***

Working on the Subconscious Level
Our second method is: ***Prove It to Yourself.*** Start proving it to yourself that you are worthy of success. How? Be good to other people. Watch yourself being good to other people. Do helpful actions whether it's simply opening a door for someone or helping a child with homework.

If you're selling something, make sure that the person has a good buying experience. After a week, I'm still telling people about my good experience created by an expert salesman who sold me my recent suits.

Tell stories about how you're helping people. When you talk about how you've helped someone, you're programming yourself on the subconscious level that you ARE a good person doing good!

3. Clear the feeling that one's success "takes away" from someone else

Have you met some people who seemed to be stuck in "scarcity thinking"? From the way they talk, it seems they are trying to push the *supposition* that anyone's good fortune takes away from others.

However, when people actually take time to study the efforts of a number entrepreneurs, they uncover many projects that have *significantly improved the lives of many people!*

For example, Sara Blakely came up with the idea Spanx, known as an undergarment that gives the wearer a slim and shapely appearance.

Based on her ingenuity and efforts, Sara became a billionaire. Did she take away anything? No. She came up with an idea and put people to work, and she gave many women a feeling that they looked better. Spanx became so pervasive that it was featured in the movie *The Heat*. Sandra Bullock's character was wearing Spanx and said, "They're my Spanx. They hold everything together."

Further, Sara established The Sara Blakely Foundation to help women through education and entrepreneurial training. Sara also donated $1 million to the Oprah Winfrey Leadership Academy for Girls in South Africa.

This is just one of many examples with regards to people doing good and reaping the rewards of abundance.

Working on the Subconscious Level

Our third method is: **Replace Inky Water.** The process helps you force out limiting beliefs.

Imagine that you have a bucket of clear water, but you contaminate it with ink, and soon all the water appears black.

One way to clear out the bucket would be to pour in clear water consistently until all the inky water is forced out.

We use this metaphor by identifying the inky water as contaminated thinking made of limiting beliefs. At this moment, we're targeting the limiting belief that "one's success takes away from someone else."

When we examine the Law of Attraction in action, we can find numerous examples of entrepreneurs developing new ideas, new markets, new jobs, and other new opportunities.

This also reminds me of individuals who complain that actor Robert Downey, Jr. did not "deserve" to earn $50 million for his role as Iron Man in *Marvel's The Avengers*, a film that earned $1.5 billion. A journalist calculated that with all the people who saw the film, Robert Downey, Jr. earned $0.25 per person. Considering the entertainment value he brought to the project, is it okay that he earned 25 cents per person?

People on track to receive abundance and welcome opportunities via the Law of Attraction tend to reply, "Yes!"

How much does Robert Downey, Jr. give to charity? Who knows?

However, it's been reported that Angelina Jolie uses this plan: 1/3 of her income goes to charity, 1/3 goes to savings and 1/3 she lives on with her family.

Many of us would say, "Sounds good."

The method of *Replace Inky Water* is to keep filling your mind with positive examples and thoughts about abundance. Such positive material is clear water replacing inky water, and in turn, abundance thinking replacing scarcity thinking. **In doing so, we notice that there are people who innovate and keep making the "pie" [what's available to people] bigger and bigger.**

In essence, when I'm talking about the strategy Replace Inky Water, I'm inviting you to gather the evidence and convince yourself that more abundance can be made.

Here's another example. Before 1995's *Toy Story*, there had been no feature length computer-animated films.

In 1995, *Toy Story* earned $361.9 million. It opened a new form of entertainment.

In the year, 2012, there were several computer-animated films from various studios:

2012 (computer animated films' earnings):
Brave - $539 million
Wreck-It Ralph - $471.2 million
Hotel Transylvania - $385.3 million
Rise of the Guardians - $306.9 million
Ice Age 4 - $877.2 million
The Lorax - $348.8 million

Madagascar 3 - $746.9 million

The above shows that the "pie" or levels of abundance can expand and expand.

The person who wants the Law of Attraction to flow in his or her life will take the above details and realize they support abundance thinking. You can consistently use abundance thinking to persistently replace the stagnant effects of scarcity thinking.

How will *you* consistently and daily fill your mind with "the clear water of abundance thinking"?

4. Clear the feeling of fear of losses that may come with success

Several years ago, I had a particular close friend "Bob" who dropped a few of his friends. I watched this and a clear *intuitive thought* came to me: "Bob is going to drop me when one of my entrepreneurial projects brings in big income. He'll make up some reason to be mad at me and then he'll disappear from my life."

I expressed my concern to Bob and surprise—he did *not* say, "No, Tom. That won't happen."

A couple of months later, he dropped me even *before* my big project-success.

I really grieved about Bob disappearing from my life: We had been friends for over 21 years. There were many good times, but the friendship was no more.

My point with sharing this story is: I learned something important:

Some friendships are like novels.

Some friendships are like short stories.

And some friendships are a sentence. (Put a period on that thing and get away!)

My point is that when I took a close look at my relationship with Bob, I realized that he, at times, would tear down my entrepreneurial efforts. So ultimately, it was a relief to lose Bob from my life.

I'll put this in a few words: as you become successful, you will lose a few things—and, most likely, a few friendships.

But being yourself and living on your true path is worth it!

Besides, we all lose things and people on the path.

Just two months ago, a close friend, Harry, died. I lost him. Today, I caught myself automatically dialing his phone number. I stopped dialing.

The week of his death, I called Harry's voicemail system to hear his voice. His outgoing voicemail message sounded like he was bored and tired. That was *not* my friend!

So I let it go. I did *not* record that message. I let go of trying to hold on to some remnant of my dear friend.

You see, we all flow thorough different "chapters" in our lives. It helps to practice letting go.

As you become more and more successful, you enter new chapters in life and some people will not want to go into the new chapter with you.

Consider developing yourself so you feel strong and able to withstand the losses that may come with success—and feel sure that the losses "make space" for better people, things and opportunities to now fit into your life.

I know this can be hard. At times, I still feel sad that a chapter (with my friendship with Bob) *closed* in my life. But here's the crucial detail: Would I go back? No!

The answer to the fear of about success and related losses is to add a new empowering thought—or what I call the **Empowered Link.**

Working on the Subconscious Level
Our fourth method is: **Add the Empowered Link**.

A number of long-time practitioners of meditation (such as Buddhist monks) report that they avoid thoughts of suffering. That is, after years and thousands of hours of meditation, they rarely think disquieting thoughts.

Personally, I have NOT meditated enough to avoid having disquieting thoughts. The majority of my clients have not risen to the "monk-level of meditating."

So what do we do with disquieting thoughts?

We can use the method of the *Empowered Link*.

A disquieting thought arises and you *Link* an *Empowering Thought* to it. In essence, you "cancel out" the first thought, which is harmful, and replace it with a thought that is empowering.

Researchers suggest that we have 12,000 to 70,000 thoughts per day. Much of these thoughts are automatic, negative, "re-run" thoughts. They're just conditioned thoughts that pop up whenever a present stimulus is similar to a stimulus from our past.

For example, when I was in 7th grade, I went to a classmate "Susan" and asked, "Can I walk you home?"

She replied with a sneer, "What for?!" In front of her sister. I ran home, lost my keys during that run and got in big trouble. I never found the keys.

It would have been easy to let the disquieting thought: "Beware of all girls with long, brown hair and glasses!" run my life.

Instead, I learned to have the Empowering Thought: *"I'm talking to a new person here. This is a new moment."*

Doing so, empowered me to not shy away from the rejection one might endure in the pursuit of love, and I was *not* prevented from having girlfriends in my later years.

I'm suggesting that *you pay attention* to your disquieting thoughts and make an Empowered Link.

Here's another example: Years ago, any time I would complain about a particular job I did just to earn rent money, I would immediately add this *Empowered Thought:* "I am grateful for steady work."

Immediately, I felt better!

So in this section, we're talking about the disquieting thought: "If I'm successful, I'm going to lose something or someone."

You could develop your own Empowered Link: *"Losses may happen, but that makes space for better opportunities and good people in my life."*

You could use another version: *"I can handle it. More opportunities and people are waiting to greet me!"*

Now it's your turn.

How can you add an *Empowered Link* (or automatic empowered thought) to any recurring fearful thought you may have about becoming successful?

Remember the Empowered Link process is about consciously choosing to add an Empowered Thought to any recurring fearful thought. In this way, you avoid blocking the flow that the Law of Attraction has to offer. You, by your own self-chosen conditioning, place yourself into an empowered state of being.

5. Clear the "hesitation block" and feel (everyday) a Deep Need to do what's necessary to succeed

What is holding many people back from more success? They do *not* feel a Deep Need to do what's necessary to succeed.

This is a profound realization.

We're not goofing around here. We are not talking about having a wish to have a little more money. *We **are** talking about making big, meaningful improvements in life and happiness!*

In my book, *Reduce Clutter, Enlarge Your Life*, I shared this story:

"My client, Joseph, rented a large storage locker filled with junk—for 20 years. His wife occasionally complained about the expense.

Joseph worked long hours and explained that he did not have the energy or time to devote to reducing the amount of junk in his storage locker.

Then one day, he read a paragraph of a book that showed how one can lose thousands of dollars over a span of years while renting a storage locker. In essence, one pays so much rent that one could buy the objects 20 times over.

I asked Joseph to literally calculate how much money he would save if he reduced the size of his storage locker down to a 4 x 5 locker for only $64.00 per month.

He calculated that he could save $4,944.00 in a couple of years.

Still he was not moved.

Then, Joseph told me that one of his family members expressed her big wish was to go to Walt Disney World in 2017 and see James Cameron's Avatarland (based on the blockbuster feature film *Avatar*).

I invited Joseph to focus on the possibility of making his loved one's dream come true. "Think of how $4,944 will help you make a family trip possible," I said.

Boom! Now, Joseph had a **Huge Reason** to tackle the hassle of getting rid of a bunch of junk.

He immediately took action that day and rented the $64.00 storage locker and moved 5 boxes of "definitely keep" material into the new storage locker."

Upon additional reflection, I realized multiple principles involved in the above story:

Not only did Joseph have a Huge Reason, he also *had a Deep Need* to do his best in making life good and happy for his loved one.

You can read all the books and try different methods for a month or two to increase your income, but you may not make a break through. And that is because you may not possess in your mind a Deep Need to do what is necessary to succeed.

To have the Law of Attraction flow well in your life, you need to AIM IT at something that you feel deeply in your heart!

That's what I'm referring to with the story of Joseph taking massive action to make the dream of his family member come true.

To be rich, you cannot be normal. – Noah St. John

So-called "normal" or "average" people, will simply not do what committed professionals will do.

They won't rehearse for hours; they won't study daily; they won't bear the price of scorn by friends and family.

I'm am not saying that living your best life is easy. I AM saying that it's worth it . . . when you connect with your Deep Need.

For many of us, our Deep Need is to be good to a loved one or perhaps, a cause.

And many of us are similar: We'll do more for someone else than ourselves.

And then, there are entrepreneurs who simply want to see an idea become reality in the world. Steve Jobs said, "I want to put a dent in the universe."

Recently, I read *Think and Grow Rich for Women*, the expanded version of the original book, *Think and Grow Rich* by Napoleon Hill. In her book for women, author Sharon Lechter shared that every day she does 2-2-2 . . . that's two emails, two handwritten notes and two posts in social media. In this way she is always filling "the pipeline" — that is, she is always attracting new business.

I have a question. What Deep Need would move you to adopt a discipline like Sharon's "2-2-2"?

Working on the Subconscious Level

Our fifth method is: **Face the Reality of Your Deep Need.**

One of my Deep Needs has its genesis in my facing tough times immediately upon graduating from college.

I needed to swiftly raise money to fund a feature film that I was going to direct. Back then, we did *not* have Amazon, Wikipedia and other resources. There was no Linkedin, Facebook or Kickstarter to connect with anyone. I wasn't even in Los Angeles. Instead, I was in a little town in Northern California.

I did NOT know what to do. I was terrified and desperate. I had some people with me but everyone turned to me to pull off the miracle of getting strangers to invest in an unknown director (me) and an unknown team. It was one of the lowest points of my life. I retreated. I'd write the screenplay all night long, awaken late in the day, and feel relieved that I didn't have to confront strangers that day. It was already 5 pm so I was "off the hook."*

[*Several years later, I wrote the book that I really needed back when I had just graduated; I titled it: *Darkest Secrets of Making a Pitch for the Film and Television Industry: How You Can Get a Studio Executive, Producer, Name Actor or Private Investor to Say "Yes" to Your Project.*]

Even so I was at a complete loss. I was desperate; I didn't know where to turn. So this terribly painful experience inspired one of my Deep Needs . . .

One of my Deep Needs is to be equipped and armed for the tough battles of life.

So everyday, I study—reading books and new articles about various aspects of business, deal-making, team leadership and more.

I refuse to be caught again (like in my twenties) without a bunch of case histories and principles in my mind so that I will have an edge in whatever next business challenge I face.

Each year, I read many books (74 books in 2015) to keep up and stay prepared.

Now, it's your turn.

What has really hurt you? Where are the sources of your Deep Needs?

Can you use the past pain as *Present Fuel* so you'll do what's necessary to succeed today and tomorrow?

Every top successful person I have interviewed has demonstrated that they are fueled by both positive intentions and also Deep Needs to overcome past pain.

I always remember one particular case history I read more than ten years ago.

Back in the 50's, a new bride went to her husband and asked for $10.00.

"What for?" her husband demanded.

"Nothing," she said, offended. From that moment forward, she resolved to never ask him for money again.

She got a job and then started her own business and became prosperous with her own efforts. Good for her!

And, we can see that her success was in part fueled by her past pain and her Deep Need to be independent and never humiliated about money again!

Now, let's shift gears. A Deep Need may be fueled by a positive intention. For example, as I mentioned earlier, a number of us will do more for someone we love than for ourselves. You can use that as your Deep Need to do what's necessary to succeed.

Pull out a sheet of paper or type into a laptop, *what deeply moves you to action.*

The sooner you get clear on this, the more powerful you become in using it and the faster you get at moving forward.

I call the above details the process of *Face the Reality of Your Deep Need.* For many of us, the underlying cause for us to get into action may *not* be something we want to discuss at the dinner table.

Use the truth about yourself to take action and open the door for the Law of Attraction to *really* work in your life.

* * *

In summary, here are the methods to help you remove the blocks so the Law of Attraction functions well in your life:

1. Replace the Stuck Story
2. Prove It to Yourself
3. Replace Inky Water
4. Add the Empowered Link
5. Face the Reality of Your Deep Need

Principle
Free up your possibilities. Replace limiting beliefs with the true power of your Deep Need. Use discipline to get your brain to serve you in better ways.

Power Questions
What personal stories (and case histories) inspire you?

How can you prove it to yourself that your success is already helping others?

What limiting beliefs do you want to crowd out of your mind?

What Empowered Thought do you want linked to a recurring fearful thought you have?

How can you use your Deep Need to get you into consistent action?

_____

_____

_____

Law of Attraction and How You Overcome Self-Sabotage

Adriana knows that if she'd attend a networking event on Tuesday, she would increase her circle of contacts. But she engages in self-sabotage by staying awake too late on Monday night. She made herself too tired on Tuesday to attend the networking event, and so she missed her opportunity to expand her networking circle of contacts. Why did she engage in self-sabotage?

That IS the question: Why would we do self-sabotage? Much of it arises from conditioning that we endured as a younger person. As a child we do not realize the harm created by limiting beliefs (foisted on us by parents and guardians). As we grow up, the beliefs are simply what we know.

The Law of Attraction is hampered by the mixed signals we send into the universe when we're restrained by limiting beliefs, confusion and fear of uncertainty.

As I mentioned above, these are the particular, insidious elements:

1) Limiting beliefs
2) Confusion
3) Fear of uncertainty

1) Limiting beliefs

Just a few minutes ago, a friend was driving her car and said to me, "Oh, no! We're going to catch all the red lights." I replied, "I don't know that; we haven't arrived at each light yet."

A big problem with a limiting belief is that it drains your energy. The phrase "We're going to catch all the red lights" causes stress, and the phrase may be wrong!

A limiting belief can even cause you pain because a limiting belief can wind up your body with adrenaline.

One of my friends "Cindy" gets chest pains when she hears certain words. For example, she talked with her therapist and felt pain when asked, "Who are you pleasing too much?"

So Cindy holds two limiting beliefs: 1) If I take care of myself and get a few nights of relaxation, some people will not like me because I'm not helping them, and 2) my health is really fragile.

Both limiting beliefs box her in so she does not do certain activities.

In this way, limiting beliefs are a big part of her self-sabotaging actions and self-sabotaging inactivity.

The solution includes taking a good look at your beliefs. Talk about them. Ask yourself. Is this belief true for me now — as an adult? Was this belief just something I constructed when I was afraid as a child?

For example, author Lois P. Frankel wrote books called *Nice Girls Don't Get the Corner Office* and *Nice Girls Don't Get Rich*. Lois' point is that "being a nice girl" was something that was okay for childhood, but what is better now is "being a Strong Woman."

Now it's your turn.

In your journal, write down five of your beliefs. Now look at them carefully. Does each belief help you? Is the belief even true for you now? Could you hold a better belief?

Some people mindlessly parrot a comment "money is the root of all evil."

Instead of that, I say, "Money is a tool I use well for the benefit of all involved." I prefer my Expansive Belief.

2) Confusion

Confusion arises from mixed thoughts and mixed feelings. Here are examples:
- I want this, but I don't deserve it.
- I want this, but I'm afraid that things will get worse.

Sometimes, our confusion and mixed feelings lie below the surface in our subconscious mind. To get at such subconscious turmoil and to shine some light on the elements, we can talk about the details with someone we trust. We need a session in which we talk and the other person simply listens and does not offer comments. It could help if the friend or counselor writes down some notes. Then, the friend could read back something we say. This helps because sometimes we say something, but we do not really notice the kernel of truth.

Another way to get at our subconscious beliefs and

feelings is through drawing or assembling images we find in magazines. Do the process quickly and see what you find on the paper.

I once responded to a direction in a workbook: "Draw a sketch of your parents." I drew a volcano to represent my father. And I drew an invisible woman (made of dashes instead of lines) to represent my mother. I learned much from those sketches.

Now it's your turn.

Pick a method (sketch or assemble images from magazines).

See what your images bring up in terms of your feelings and thoughts.

A solution: Imagine that this is an "AND-Universe."

Here are examples:

I feel "I want this, but I don't deserve it." I can take steps forward AND I can make the project serve people. So I can get what I want AND by serving others, I will feel that the project is worthwhile.

I feel "I want this, but I'm afraid that things will get worse." I can take small steps forward. I can get expert advice. I can get training so that I'm stronger in this area of work. AND I can look at what might go wrong. AND I can take steps so I can adapt to anything that may go wrong. AND I can learn from the journey.

Write down your own "AND-possibilities."

3) Fear of uncertainty

Do the thing you fear and the death of fear is certain.
– Ralph Waldo Emerson

I've done many things that inspired fear in me: first time directing a feature film, first time giving a speech to

697 people, and first time writing a book. [One of my books helps you meet people for the first time. It's titled *Now You See Me – Make a Great First Impression – Use Secrets of Power Networking: for More Clients, More Referrals and More Friends.*]

I might hesitate to say that my fear "died."

What did die was my being sabotaged by fear. Instead of being frozen by fear, I stepped forward.

That's an important realization.

Of my 33 books, about three do not sell. So I've endured "failure" with writing a book that does not find an audience.

I've learned to face the uncertainty and NOT let the uncertainty shut down my activity or creativity.

Now it's your turn.

Does feeling uncertain and feeling fear stop you in your tracks? Is there something that you can make More Important than fear? Write your thoughts and feelings in your journal (or on these lines below)

_____

_____

"Courage is not the absence of fear but rather the judgment that something is more important than fear." – Meg Cabot

The "This or Better" Solution

If you have a spiritual path, you could say this prayer that invokes the Law of Attraction.

"Please help me make _____ happen in my life. Thank you for supporting me on this path. I want _____ . . . I want this or better. Thank you."

The idea of the Law of Attraction is that you attract

what you think about most. A good plan is to get clear on what you want and still make space so the universe delivers what you want or better.

Enjoy Enhancing Your Courage through the Law of Attraction

Imagine feeling great courage. The Law of Attraction can help you with this. For some of us, the idea of the Law of Attraction is comforting. It can be understood by thinking: "If I think positively, then positive outcomes are surely on their way to me."

The law of attraction is the attractive, magnetic power of the Universe that draws similar energies together. It manifests through the power of creation, everywhere and in multiple ways. – Remez Sasson

So the idea that the Universe will get behind you and help you manifest what you truly want can enhance your courage.

On the other hand, some people feel fear related to the ideas of the Law of Attraction. They might have certain thoughts enter their mind like this: "Wait a minute! If I'm worried about something, I will draw exactly what I fear to me!"

I've learned that while fearful thoughts do occur, the answer is to condition yourself to think empowering thoughts after a fearful thought. I call this **The Power of Your Second Thought.**

To manifest what you really want often requires courage.

I learned that courage was not the absence of fear, but the triumph over it. The brave man is not he who does not feel afraid, but he who conquers that fear. – Nelson Mandela

Here's where courage comes in. Some people think of a big, positive dream for their lives but then feel fear. "What if it doesn't work out? What if I lose money? What if I look foolish and my friends and family make fun of me?"

It takes a great deal of bravery to stand up to our enemies, but just as much to stand up to our friends. – J. K. Rowling

The courage part is to keep moving forward in spite of the fear.

To use the Law of Attraction in your favor, do take time and think of what you really want. Then do not just stay in that one mode of thinking. Start getting more information and training—and Take Action!

Now I'm going to share really practical methods. Knowing and using these practical methods will build up your positive thoughts (attracting positive outcomes).

We'll use the C.A.N. process:

C – cover the downside

A – arrange your own approval

N – nurture yourself

1. Cover the downside

Inaction breeds doubt and fear. Action breeds confidence and courage. If you want to conquer fear, do not sit home and think about it. Go out and get busy. – Dale Carnegie

Here's an important part of "getting busy."

Make a thorough plan that includes backup details to ensure your continued well-being even if something goes wrong.

Do not shy away from taking action just because you might have to face a disappointing outcome. If I do 20 projects, some of them will not yield the income that I prefer. But I move ahead anyway. How can I do that?

Each project has a budget so I can withstand a loss or two because the budget was not too big to "sink the whole company."

That's what I mean by "cover the downside": The downside would be investing money in a project and then that project does not breakeven. To cover the downside would be to strategically keep the budget low.

In essence, that's making a thorough plan that includes allowances for missteps. Having a thorough plan can boost your courage.

Successful people know and use 'the numbers.'

Another way to boost your courage is to "know the important numbers." By this I mean: identify what specific steps and items you need to improve.

Measurement is the first step that leads to control and eventually to improvement. If you can't measure something, you can't understand it. If you can't understand it, you can't control it. If you can't control it, you can't improve it.

– H. James Harrington

Successful people know how much income must be brought in by sales to breakeven and to go into profit.

They know, on average, how many marketing phone calls lead to gaining a new client.

Here's where you boost your courage. If you don't measure things, you will likely have "free floating anxiety" because so many things will be uncertain.

On the other hand, as soon as you write a plan on paper and take some action, you'll feel stronger. Your courage will expand.

Such good thoughts and good feelings, by the Law of Attraction, will bring you better and better results.

2. Arrange your own approval

Let's return to this quote: *It takes a great deal of bravery to stand up to our enemies, but just as much to stand up to our friends. – J. K. Rowling*

I have had friends who could NOT see my vision for projects. They warned me against moving forward. If I had listened to them, I would have been stopped in my tracks. Some projects like my book *Darkest Secrets of Persuasion and Seduction Masters: How to Protect Yourself and Turn the Power to Good* have yielded income every month. So those particular friends were *wrong!*

What happened then? They merely shrugged and said something like: "Oh, well. Some things turn out okay."

Okay! They almost led me down the path of doing nothing and helping nobody. That's serious.

So I invite you to avoid living for anyone else's approval. **Set your own internal and personal standards.** In essence, "arrange your own approval."

3. Nurture yourself

Acting in a courageous manner takes energy and internal reserves. How do you have such reserves? You nurture yourself. I've said to clients: *Take breaks or be broken.*

When you nurture yourself, you build up your resilience. To manifest your dreams you need a big helping of resilience! When you stretch and grow, you'll have some projects and some experiences that really disappoint you. But you can be proud of yourself that you demonstrated courage. You took an appropriate risk. Good for you!

To really get the Law of Attraction working for you, approach your activities with strategy. Use strategy in how you think (habitually) and how you make plans and take action.

Your courage will expand and the Law of Attraction will assist you in manifesting terrific outcomes.

Principle
Enhance the Law of Attraction working *for* you by taking courageous action.

Power Question
How can you nurture yourself so you have the energy to take courageous action?

_____

_____

_____

Raise Your Confidence through the Law of Attraction

Want to feel really confident? You *can!* Use the Law of Attraction to do just that. How? I'll illustrate this with a story.

Some years ago, I was casting a feature film. I was directing test footage with a young woman "Ginny" who was auditioning. Ginny turned and her shimmering blond hair flowed. She moved with grace—born of her years as both gymnast and dancer.

In the scene, I was acting, portraying the hero who had no idea that this young woman was from the future. (This was a scene from a screenplay, later a book, I wrote entitled *TimePulse**.

* *TimePulse: Beyond Titanic* has a free chapters at Amazon.com

When the camera rolls, any actor can have a degree of fear.

But as a *trained* actor I had an advantage. I was trained to use "the objective." Often as a director, I have asked an actor, "In this moment, what do you want?" The answer "I want____" is the objective.

One of the tough things for an actor to do convincingly is to listen in a scene. If the actor effectively uses *the objective*, he can be real. How? In any moment—in real life—we want something.

So using my objective, I was confident in the scene. I acted *without* novice-actor nervousness.

In the scene, I was completely connected to what the character wants moment to moment.

The videotaped audition went well, and I was clear about what I wanted both as director and producer.

Such confidence was attractive.

In real life, Ginny soon became my girlfriend.

So let's discuss the essence of confidence as expressed in the above story.

Clarity and connection to what you really want often comes across as confidence.

Frankly, it's a real cliché about good directors: "Yes, she really knew what she wanted."

Here's where the Law of Attraction and confidence mix together.

The Law of Attraction often waits for you to express clarity about what you want. No hesitation. No shyness. Ask for what you want. Focus on what you want.

And if appropriate keep these thoughts to yourself.

Especially do *not* mention your big dreams to pessimists who cannot even imagine that big dreams come true. Such pessimists look upon the achievers of the world as "freaks of nature" or "merely lucky freaks."

The basic form of using the Law of Attraction is *Ask, Believe Receive*. And I celebrate the "ask" part. It's like using *the objective* which is found by answering the question: "What do you want?"

But it's not merely a quiet "What do you want?"

No! It's a loud, powerful *"What do you REALLY want?"*

That's when you engage the Law of Attraction. You proclaim to yourself (and in your mind, to the universe): "I REALLY want _____."

So many of us fail to truly engage the Law of Attraction because we're afraid to hope and we're afraid to get our hopes dashed. I invite you let go of trying to protect yourself from disappointment.

The truth is: If you try to shield yourself from disappointment—disappointment in life will come anyway!

Instead, *decide now* to let yourself Want what you Want. Let go of having to know how you'll get your desire—instead acknowledge your deep desire and take appropriate action.

Now, will you always get what you want?

The answer is in three parts:
- a) sometimes you get what you want in exactly the form you envision it
- b) sometimes you get what you want in a BETTER form that you didn't imagine
- c) sometimes you do not get what you want but you get something that deepens you as a human being so *you* become better.

Ginny and I parted ways after a time. But I continue to admire her spirit. She told me that she wanted to sing the lead role of Christine in *The Phantom of the Opera* musical. Alas, she was tone deaf. But I admired that she stayed in musical theater as a dancer.

And let's note this: What was her objective?—"I WANT to perform!"

And she got those opportunities over and over—as a dancer.

In summary, to raise your confidence level and to invoke the Law of Attraction do these things (along the lines of Ask, Believe, Receive):

- Find and acknowledge your objective [your "Want!"] and ASK.
- "Believe!"—that is envision how great you feel as if you are already receiving what you want
- Receive the blessing

A final comment about confidence:

I've done many things that scared me (directing feature films, guest-lecturing at Stanford University, acting as a lead actor in feature films). I've learned that my confidence did not rise from "comfort." No. It rose from my objective (deep desire), rehearsal, training, and from developing ways to be flexible and to adapt.

But the secret is: Confidence in my ability to adapt came from *the great personal energy provided by my Big Want.*

I wanted something So Much that I put in the work (rehearsal, study, more) to do my best.

And each time, the Law of Attraction would give me blessings.

Principle
Focus on what you want and use that energy for training and rehearsal.

Power Questions
What training/coaching could help you leap forward to more prosperity and abundance?

Action and the Law of Attraction

(I first released this below material at my blog: www.BeHeardandBeTrusted.com)

Imagine using the Law of Attraction and really improving your life! I'm not talking about just using the steps of "Ask, Believe, Receive." Why? Because a lot of people have started and stayed with "Ask, Believe, Receive" and they've been *really disappointed*.

Why did those three steps by themselves fail to produce the results people desperately crave? Consider a revision to "Ask, Believe, TAKE EFFECTIVE ACTION, Receive."

Sure, the Law of Attraction rests on "similar energies are drawn together." Hold positive thoughts and enjoy positive results.

Let's focus deeper on this. To say this in few words, many positive results have manifested for me with positive thoughts PLUS positive action. *[This is where the Law of Creation enhances how the Law of Attraction works in your life.]*

One time, I took action to direct a feature film and this

led to an unforeseen positive result. During that time, an opportunity arose for me to have a conversation on the set with an actor's father. The result? I was given a contact that led to over $331,453. Do you notice the details: if I didn't say YES to direct the film or if I did not *do* well in directing the film, I would not have had that crucial conversation!

So repeat with me: "Ask, Believe, TAKE EFFECTIVE ACTION, Receive."

I invite you to ask yourself: "Where am I *not* taking action? What small action can I take so that I can start the flow of positive opportunities in my direction? Then, do MORE than have positive thoughts: Take Positive Action.

Recently, in a class, I replied to a question by saying, "I'm an OptiRealist. Take your optimism plus realism and then you can win." [OptiRealist.com]

When I say "win," I mean enjoy success, joy and fulfillment. Often, there can be multiple winners. In my work, there can be multiple effective speakers, authors and producers. I realize that in the world of sports, there is one gold medalist for a particular sport. However, much of what we do provides us with opportunities beyond being "one winner." And thank goodness!

So let's return to "Ask, Believe, TAKE EFFECTIVE ACTION, Receive." The universe is waiting to see if you're serious about something. Will you study, rehearse, or get coaching? And will you "put yourself into the arena"? That is, will you go make the presentation to potential investors? Will you ask a person for a date? Will you complete your book and see that it's available on Amazon?

Recently, a friend said, "It's not about wishing for more money, it's about saying a prayer that you become better at what you do. Then more money comes in naturally."

From that conversation, I coined a phrase: "It's not about asking for gifts; it's about increasing your capacity." That is, increase your capacity to effectively serve others, and the universe will naturally bring rewards and opportunities to you. You are then attractive. Now, that's the Law of Attraction in action!

Principle
Use action [the Law of Creation] to enhance how the Law of Attraction works in your life.

Power Questions
What small action can you take to move in the direction of your dreams?

Handle Anger through the Law of Attraction

Would you like less trouble and anger in your life? Fortunately, through certain actions and the Law of Attraction you can become skilled at dealing with anger.

First, I'm going to get to the heart of the matter: *Anger arises from fear.* In previous books, I've written that "Anger is fear twisted."

I've learned that if I'm angry, I am likely afraid that something bad is happening or is going to happen. I am concerned that someone I love will get hurt or I'll get hurt.

For example, many years ago, someone smashed into the little Toyota truck that my sweetheart had borrowed from her parents.

That night, I was shocked that a big Ford F-150 truck backed into and crushed the end of the *parked*, little Toyota truck. The F-150 truck backed up and slammed into the little truck a *second time*.

I was scared for my sweetheart's feelings. She would be distraught: A hit-and-run vehicle would leave my sweetheart at odds with her parents.

So I immediately ran toward the offending vehicle that was seeking to *leave the scene*. Next thing, the F-150 truck hit me in the chest, and in desperation, I was clinging to the hood of the vehicle—the driver *still* trying to leave the scene.

I yelled for help, hoping someone in the Telegraph Hill neighborhood of San Francisco would hear me, somehow intervene, and call for the police!

This was the most *terrifying moment* of my life. I thought, "What will this crazy man do next? I'll be dead if I fall off and he runs me over. He might run me over on purpose!"

Finally, the police arrived and ultimately, after legal proceedings, compensation for the little Toyota truck came through. But was the cost of my jumping in front of the offender worth it?

One smashed little Toyota truck and an F-150 hitting me in the chest. Any ordinary person would have brought the F-150 to a stop after the initial collision with the Toyota truck. But that didn't happen, and I put my life in unnecessary jeopardy.

My *fear* of my sweetheart being hurt, led to *my anger*

and to my action.

Would I do the same thing now? No. Risking death-by-truck is *not* my style of living now!

Money can be replaced, not a human life.

* * *

Anger can lead to a bad reaction.

Instead, to really invoke the Law of Attraction, you want to be in a better state of being, one of calmness. From a state of calmness, you can respond in a thoughtful and wise manner.

Here's where the Law of Attraction also comes in. If you keep focusing on fear, you keep attracting things to be afraid about. Also, anger often involves being judgmental toward another person. We judge them as doing something wrong.

And by the Law of Attraction, the more we practice being judgmental—the more we attract judgmental people into our lives. Watch out for that!

So the solution is a combination of compassion and discernment.

When you live most of your day in compassion, you are in a calm state of being. In such a state, you can practice discernment.

Often when I talk with clients and my college students, the word *discernment* is not an immediate part of their vocabulary.

I'll make certain distinctions here:

Discernment: a flexible approach. You observe what works and what does *not*. Then, you make good decisions regarding your next actions.

Judgment: a rigid approach in which one sets oneself

as superior to the other person.

Again, by the Law of Attraction, the more we practice being judgmental, the more judgmental people we attract to us. Not good.

Instead, it's better to practice *discernment*. Do not settle for your instant, reflexive judgments about a person or situation.

Learn to practice shifting to a compassionate approach.

For example, as I type this into my mini-laptop, I'm being bumped by two things: a) the rocking of the train I'm traveling in and b) the annoying sounds of a married couple grumbling to each other. I can even hear the growling couple through the ear plugs that I'm wearing.

Wife: Oh, I spent that money.
Husband: You spent it on yourself [with a pushy tone]
Wife: Yeah.
Husband: On *personal* things.

Now, my instant thoughts include: "Why is it bad to spend money on yourself? Doesn't this guy know that it's good to nurture yourself? By the way, his cross-examining his wife is not smart. He is not honoring her."

But immediately, I remind myself to be compassionate. Maybe this couple is working their way through a process. Maybe they need to *talk through* money expenditures because they've gone through *some money troubles* recently.

In any case, I remind myself that I do not know them and we humans are just trying to do the best we can, with what we know in the moment.

This example illustrates another point: it's true that we can often shift to being kind and compassionate toward a stranger, but if a loved one does something that is hurtful—it hurts double! And we often get angry.

Why? Family members are supposed to know us, and so our expectations in how we're treated are more sensitive. We have thoughts like: "You're my brother, you're supposed to be good to me!"

With compassion, however, we can view the situation as: "I prefer you to be kind to me, but you may be hurting so much (or you may be confused) that I'm *not* really in your mind at the moment. There is no room to think about how this situation affects me."

Years ago, Richard Carlson, author of *Don't Sweat the Small Stuff*, told me, "It's not that I don't get stressed out. It's that I do NOT spend much time there."

Similarly, it is good for us to learn to spend more of our day in a mode of compassion and discernment—and then we're likely to avoid pouring gasoline on small fires of irritation. In this way, we avoid igniting big flames of anger.

In a way, anger can be something that we "practice." In order to avoid, getting angry, it helps to practice something opposite: the calmness of compassion.

We do that by conditioning ourselves with compassionate thoughts.

Here are examples:

Judgmental Thought: That guy is being stupid.

Compassionate Thought: I don't know him. Maybe he's getting a divorce and he's distraught.

Judgmental Thought: That person is talking loud in his own language.

Compassionate Thought: Maybe that person has had some hearing loss. I bet my language sounds strange to him, too.

Judgmental Thought: What a mean thing to say!

Compassionate Thought: Maybe my family member is

not trying to be mean. Maybe she's just tired.

Remember, to really get the Law of Attraction flowing well in your life, spend more of your day in a compassionate state of being.

Principle
When judgmental thoughts arise, shift to discernment, be flexible and make good choices.

Power Questions
What are some judgmental thoughts you have often? What would help you make a shift in your thoughts? Taking a breath? (Perhaps, you might tell yourself: "I shift from judgment to discernment.")

_____

_____

_____

Handle Loss through the Law of Attraction

Some people are concerned that they're not "doing it right" if they experience grief when loss befalls them.

Actually—when grief occurs, it can happen because the Law of Attraction brought you high quality friends or high quality projects.

Of course, if a friend dies or another friend drifts away, it's supposed to hurt because you had something *valuable* in your life!

So how do you deal with grief in a "Law of Attraction friendly way"?

You learn to flow from moment to moment.

You avoid staying stuck.

On a given day, you may experience tears a number of times. Each time may be for part of an hour. And still, a few moments may actually bring you some instants of laughter.

Good! *You're stepping into each moment fresh.*

Some years ago, I was teaching a class of graduate students and I choked up. Just the day before, I learned that a close friend had committed suicide.

So I said to the students, "A close friend of mine has died. I might get choked up for 30 seconds. But things are okay. We'll flow forward soon."

Everything worked out. I even saw some students nod. They connected with me person to person.

The universe wants to bring you more friends and more projects.

So show the universe that you welcome it all: the joys, the highs, the lows and the grief when necessary.

Stay in the moment and remember to turn the direction of your thoughts by saying, "I'm grateful for ____." Fill in the blank with whatever warms your heart.

About projects: it's natural to feel some emptiness when a good project comes to completion.

The solution is to "overlap projects." Start another project *before* the ending of your current project. In this way you avoid a big dip in energy as you grieve over the ending of the first project.

Remember, step into each moment fresh.

Principle
Handle loss by learning to keep "in the flow."
Power Questions
How can you enter each moment fresh? Are you getting enough sleep? Do you take good care of yourself? Do you allow yourself to "feel it all"—to feel the joy, the sorrow, and the love?

Handle Disappointment through the Law of Attraction

Have you thought that if you "did the Law of Attraction right" that you could avoid disappointment? I can help with this perception.

Every person who has had a major impact on world culture has endured BIG disappointments.

Thomas Edison's first patent yielded a product that the Congress shunned. He designed a device that could record a senator's vote quickly. But the Congress did NOT want that! They wanted to do backroom deals instead. So Edison faced big disappointment. Historians have said that this led to Edison always searching for a target market *first* before sinking effort and funds into a project.

Steve Jobs once tried to sell a computer named Lisa. People said that it cost too much and it did too little. The Lisa computer just disappeared into history without notice.

Walt Disney's first two companies went bankrupt.

Several years ago, Oprah Winfrey lost her new broadcasting anchor position because she reported the news with "too much emotion." That was a big disappointment for her!

Then she landed the host position for a show called "People Are Talking," and she said, "It was like coming home."

Oprah's TV program "The Oprah Winfrey Show" remains the highest-rated talk show in American television history. It did well for 25 seasons.

More recently, Oprah's cable channel OWN debuted to terrible ratings. In fact, she said that she was embarrassed to give a speech at Harvard University around that time. She felt like she was really failing. As of 2012 the OWN channel's losses were estimated as $330 million. Let's remember that Oprah is a billionaire, so she can take the hit, but the loss still hurts.

Oprah is likely to improve the network or do something different. I am *not* worried for her.

My point is: Doing the Law of Attraction "right" is NOT about avoiding all disappointment. *It's about attracting the experiences and resources that make you strong and truly capable of making great decisions at a particular time.*

If you feel big disappointment, some of those experiences are based on when you had something really good and then it went away.

Two of my friendships ended and I still grieve about them—when I think about them. But I am grateful that those friendships enhanced earlier chapters of my life

You see *I did have the Law of Attraction working well in my life:* I attracted those two friendships at *just the right time* to be good to those people—and they were kind to me.

To make this clear:

When the Law of Attraction is working well in your life, it's about JUST THE RIGHT TIME. You attract what you need for this chapter in your life. Sure things will change in later months or years. You can feel disappointed. That is okay. Not fun. But appropriate for one's journey in life.

As one of my editors suggested: "Sometimes losing something, like a friend who cuts you down, is a *good* thing!"

Be observant to see the big picture. Look for opportunities to say, "I am grateful for _____."

This keeps the Law of Attraction flowing well in your life.

Principle

Look at the big picture and frequently say, "I am grateful for _____."

Power Questions

What is working in your life? What are you grateful for? What gratitude-practice can you implement in your life? (You might want to list three positive details/occurrences from your day in a Gratitude Journal just before you go to sleep each night.)

The Law of Attraction and Your Feeling Good!

Do you remember a time when you felt great!? Some of us are out of practice in terms of feeling good.

Does this sound like you? Are you all clogged up with worrying and being busy?

Good moments can arrive but we may not make space for them. For example, a moment ago I was brushing my teeth getting ready to go to bed.

But then some ideas for this section leapt into my mind. Did I shrug and let the opportunity to write these words evaporate? No! I leapt to the computer and started typing. *And I feel great.*

Also, I know what images instantly put me in a good mood. For example, I always feel good when I arrive outside Disneyland and see the top of the Matterhorn Mountain—visible above the trees that obscure the park from the street. It always reminds me: "I'm here at Disneyland!"

To really get the Law of Attraction working well, you need to become clear within your own self. In a way, you are "aiming" the Law of Attraction on your behalf. In fact, that's part of the "ask, believe, receive" idea within the Law of Attraction. *You need to ask for what you want.*

Here's another idea about feeling good. You need to look for *many ways* that will likely get you what you want.

For example, at this time, I don't have the opening in my schedule to be in Disneyland each month. However, when I walk down the main street of a nearby California town, I feel good. Why? This town has lights in their trees (just like Disneyland's Main Street U.S.A.)! So when I'm walking in that town, I can make a switch in my mind and look upon the world in a special way: seeing the magic.

I now invite you to write down in your journal those moments you have enjoyed.

My clients have noted:
- listening to music
- swing dancing
- tai chi
- reading a good book

Remember, do you homework. To really have the Law of Attraction flowing in your life, learn what you really like and what gets you to feel good.

In this way, your "message to the universe" will be clear, "I'll have more of these magic moments, please. Thank you!"

Principle

To attract more times when you feel good, identify what you enjoy doing and experiencing.

Power Questions

Can you recall some of the moments in your life when you felt good? How could you bring moments like these into your present life?

Have Some Targets and the Law of Attraction Helps You Reach Them

Below I'm including one of my articles from my blog at

www.BeHeardandBeTrusted.com.

This particular blog article arose from my intuition and a strange experience I lived through. This relates to the Law of Attraction in that *we need to have some real targets in order for the Law of Attraction operate well in our lives."*

"I was Tweeted by a Dead Man" and Insights on Life

A tweet from Joe?! I was shocked. He had been dead over a month. Joe's Hollywood business manager had alerted me to Joe's passing after I had called Joe repeatedly but had only heard his outgoing voicemail message.

Joe's business manager assured me that police officers had entered Joe's home and found him dead.

But still I received a tweet. I studied the tweet and realized that it was likely Joe's Twitter account was somehow connected to a feed from another person's account. I admit that I felt a gut-punch of grief on realizing that Joe really was gone.

I know a couple of people who have died but their Facebook wall remains visible. Now, on a deceased person's wall, you can see "R.I.P" (rest in peace) in messages left by bereaved loved ones.

You can see what the dead person was posting and commenting on in their last days of life.

Yesterday, I finished reading *Jim Henson: The Biography*—a good book. The leader behind the success of the Muppets died at 53 years old.

Do you think about your legacy? Who will remember you? What good will outlive you?

This is important.

At one point, a guy I'll call "Stephen" told me about how upset he was with God. Stephen had attended all the services and done all of the rituals required by his religion. But Stephen was *not* getting what he wanted. He was mad!

I then had a thought. I said to Stephen, *"Maybe, you need someone new to serve."*

(In recent years, Stephen had been isolating himself. He was not engaged with people and so his life was bereft of the *blessings of good feelings that people have when they're being helpful to others.*)

Researchers have verified that people tend to feel better when they feel valuable to the lives of others.

I invite you to find some way to be helpful to others. For example, my company Tom Marcoux Media, LLC holds to this mission: *"We create energizing, encouraging edutainment for our good and humankind's rise."*

You don't need to have a company to focus on service.

Stay observant, and listen to your intuition.

For example, this morning, I woke up with the thought that I had not finished reading the book, The Disneyland Encyclopedia.

Later, I walked into a particular room and happened to find the book in a pile of other books.

Then I read a paragraph in this book that included a mention of "Sam," someone I know.

I thought about sending Sam an email and telling him the good news that he and his one-man show were referenced in the book.

Then, I opened my email and found a note from Linkedin.com that alerted me that *today is Sam's birthday*. So I sent him a happy birthday message that included the "gift" of telling him that he is referenced on page 101.

I shared the above example to demonstrate that we can all be kind and of service to each other—everyday.

Take good care of yourself and listen to your intuition. Watch for opportunities to be helpful.

Make your life count.

Let kindness be your legacy.

And, you'll enjoy your life today!

Principle
Find ways to be of service to people and let kindness be your legacy.

Power Questions
How can you be supportive of someone each day? Will you send helpful Internet links or something else to nurture your network of contacts?

Enhance the Blessings of the Law of Attraction—when You Improve Your "Verbal Reflexes"

"No, it won't work."

"No, I can't do that."

Do you know someone who says comments like the two above? Do you find yourself falling into reflexive comments that are negative and that drain you of energy?

I know a number of people so negative that they do not even notice the energy-draining drivel pouring from their mouths. It's like a *reflex*.

They say things like "Oh! I'm so stupid!"

"That driver is an a__h__!"

Some older people have told me, "Oh, that's not really a problem. It doesn't matter."

However, it *does* matter in two important ways:
- You drain your own energy
- You attract more negative things to you daily

1) You drain your own energy.

By the Law of Attraction, when you're judgmental and cruel toward yourself, you attract other people who are judgmental and cruel!

Why? It feels "like home." If cruelty is what you endured while growing up, it's likely that love and cruelty become twisted together. It even feels "safe" because it's familiar.

The point here is: Being reflexively negative with your words can literally drain you of energy. In many ways, there are no "neutral words." Words either build you up or tear you down.

Surround yourself with only people who are going to lift you higher. - Oprah Winfrey

Who are you around the most? YOU.

So be sure that your reflexive ways of talking build you up.

I've worked with clients with horrible, reflexive words and self-assessments.

The self-criticizers make a mistake and say: "I'm so stupid. I always f--- up. No wonder no one likes me."

On the other hand, the successful people I've interviewed say: "I made a mistake. I take responsibility. I'll do better next time. Looks like I need some coaching and rehearsal here. Okay. I've learned something."

You can see that the successful people are *coaching* themselves to do better! They don't waste time or energy on pointless self-abuse.

Realize:

Your habitual ways of talking either build you up or tear you down.

2. You attract more negative things to you daily

The rules of the Law of Attraction emphasize that what you focus on you get *more* of.

So those people who call themselves "clumsy" and klutz" attract more accidents. They keep *proving* to themselves that they are what they claim to be!

On the other hand, for years, I have purposely chosen to say, "I have an excellent memory."

For example, in a new class of college students, I call roll call and I'll celebrate that I get 22 out of 25 student's names correct during the second class.

The self-criticizer will emphasize the 3 mistakes.

Instead, I emphasize the 22 correct actions! I tell myself: "See I *do* have a good memory."

A number of authors suggest that "Life is something we co-create with God." If that's true, why would anyone want to set up a negative self-fulfilling prophesy? *Stop that.*

I once was appalled at how two generations in a family told themselves a bad story and called it the "Brown Family Bad Luck."

They said that they were in a van, the father was driving, and their van's tire suffered a blowout.

"On the freeway?" I asked.

"No, on the off-ramp."

"Anyone get hurt?"

"No. Anyway, it's our usual bad luck that we had a blowout."

I thought: "Wait a minute. Don't these people realize how lucky they were to have the blowout on *the off ramp* and to come to a *safe stop*?! No other car hit them."

The problem here is: The two parents and grown children kept telling themselves the same story of "bad luck."

That's *the opposite* of correctly enhancing the blessings of the Law of Attraction in your life. Instead, tell all of the good stories.

Take conscious choice of how *you* influence your own life. Choose your habitual words carefully. Stop cutting yourself down. Stop telling yourself "bad luck" stories.

See each blessing you have enjoyed. Tell stories about those blessings.

Lift yourself up. Coach yourself positively.

Principle
Train yourself to talk in ways that build you up.
Power Questions
What habitual sayings/stories do you express that cut you down? How can you replace such downer items with something that empowers you?

Handle Fear—and The Law of Attraction Enhances Your Life

When you handle fear and stop it from overrunning your life, the Law of Attraction can operate with more power in your favor.

A number of authors suggest that if you think about what you fear most of the time, you'll attract more of what you fear.

The solution for this situation is: Train Yourself to shift your thoughts.

It can be a simple as: "I'm afraid of having trouble during my upcoming speech. *What do I need to do well? Who can listen to me rehearse? Can I glance at a couple of books?*"

The idea is to shift from fear to *"something I can do."*

[* If you'd like a free report "9 Deadly Mistakes to Avoid for Your Next Speech and 9 Surefire Methods" — go to http://tomsupercoach.com/freereport9Mistakes4Speech.html]

For more about dealing with fear and self-doubt, we will now view a reprint of an article from my blog:

Get More Done Even when Hit with Self-Doubt and Criticism

Like a punch to my stomach, the statement from an official of the San Luis Obispo Airport rang in my ears, "You need to get your film crew out of here." We'd been filming for only one hour. As the producer-director of my first feature film, I knew that we were promised three hours.

I didn't waste a moment. I said, "Fine. We're leaving." I told my co-producer, "Have the extras leave the area. But have them walk slowly. As we go along, I'll have crew remove some movie lights." I kept filming and acting in shots while the official watched equipment and people leave. Twenty minutes later, it came down to me and one cameraman. And then we were done.

My intuition the day before yelled at me: "They might renege on the 3-hour plan." So I moved forward by storyboarding the most important shots and planned to do them first—the shots with the American Eagle airplane and the lead actors running after the plane. My intuition served me well. I listened to my gut.

Reality includes people reneging on a plan and others criticizing what you do. What's worse are the negative "voices" in our heads that bury us in self-doubt.

What's the difference that high-achievers/successful people have that people-who-are-stuck don't have? **It is the practice of stepping forward regardless of self-doubt and criticism.**

"Self-doubt is like a puppy you tuck under your arm before running across a six-lane highway." – Steve Chandler

Okay. I'm **NOT** an advocate for running across a highway. But I do see the point: *We take appropriate risks and just carry that little puppy of self-doubt with us.*

I find the above quote to inspire my freedom. Why? Because I do NOT wait for self-doubt to disappear. I press on anyway. I get coaching and I do necessary preparations and rehearsal. I say, "Courage is easier when you're prepared."

I've noticed a number of people who get stuck because they're waiting for self-doubt or lack of confidence to go away.

Do NOT let yourself to get stuck in that trap.

We'll use the N.O.W. process:

N – notice the next step and do it

O – open to coaching

W – write YOUR story

1. Notice the next step and do it

When I prepared to produce, write and direct my first feature film, I was scared. What if the film does not work? What if the crew thinks I'm too green and do not follow my directions to move fast? (Low budget filmmaking requires the team to move fast because there are so few days of filming.)

The important detail is to **Take the Next Step.**

It was easy to project into the future—that's where all of the fear lies in wait. What if the film does not turn out? What if I can't get a distributor?

Stop all of that. *Focus on the next step.* The next step is to finish the first draft of the script. Later, before the first day of filming, my next step was to personally draw 801 storyboards (illustrations). I knew exactly how one scene would transition into the next scene. I also storyboarded the complicated action scenes. How do you film landing a jets ski into the bed of a speeding truck? I figured details out in advance.

Do *not* wait to feel comfortable.

Plan your next step and take action.

2. Open to coaching

I have seen a number of episodes of the TV Show, *Restaurant Impossible*. Chef Robert Irvine arrives at a restaurant that is failing and coaches the owners to massively change their menu, working methods, leadership actions—and the restaurant gets a fantastic visual makeover!

The restaurant owners who get the most benefit are those *Open to Coaching*. The truth is they would not need Chef Robert Irvine to intervene if they really knew the best practices. Many of the restaurant owners never even worked in someone else's restaurant! How would they know what are best practices?

A phrase I use often with clients is "ALF – adapt, learn, flex."

In order to improve, we need to acknowledge that we possess weaknesses and then get coaching to improve. We will learn, adapt and flex our options. More than that, a good coach will guide us to measure our daily activities towards improvement.

"Measurement is the first step that leads to control and eventually to improvement. If you can't measure something, you can't understand it. If you can't understand it, you can't control it. If you can't control it, you can't improve it."

— H. James Harrington

I have a number of Project Logs. I note how many words a day I write and also how many pages of the trilogy of *Jack AngelSword* (graphic novels) are completed.

I invite you to get coaching, and I applaud that you're reading these words and giving me the honor to coach you at the moment.

3. Write YOUR story

Perhaps, you noticed something strange like I have. The people who yell the loudest have no experience in doing what they're criticizing.

Many times, I have taken risks to live out adventures. I have lived as an actor, lead singer/song writer, model, feature film director, guest instructor at Stanford University and more. Yet people who have never attempted such activities, threw their *negative advice* at me.

I learned to listen to my heart more than their criticisms.

It was MY story. Not their story. It was NOT their IMAGINED ideas of how to do things better, but MY ideas of how to do things better.

With my college students, I suggest: "Seek the advice of someone who has *accomplished* what you want to accomplish."

And still, you will find your OWN way of doing things.

I've reached a point where I'm comfortable in my own skin, and I do what I need to do, to feel good, but I'm built the way I am. The dancer's feet, the bruises on my legs, they're not going to go away. I think real girls have bruises. Tough chicks get bruised. They get dirty. And they have fun. - Nina Dobrev

By the way, I recall completing a film and my then-girlfriend said, "I've never seen a film like this." Okay, then. Perhaps, it works for you or it doesn't.

I find that the very things that I get criticized for, which is usually being different and just doing my own thing and just being original, is the very thing that's making me successful.

- Shania Twain

Sometimes, family members criticize what we're doing, not because they're helping us, it's because *they* do not want to feel uncomfortable. The truth is: We all get our share of disappointment. Successful people get even more disappointment because they're trying more things. Follow your heart—and get useful coaching along the way.

I learned a long time ago the wisest thing I can do is be on my own side, be an advocate for myself . . . - Maya Angelou

So I invite you to press forward even if you're criticized, even if you have self-doubt.

Take the next step.

Principle
Listen to your heart more than criticism.

Power Question
How can you remind yourself of your "first heartfelt intention." regarding a project or course of action?

The Law of Attraction and the "3 C's of Success"

One of my speech topics is "Power Up the 3 C's of Success: Charisma, Confidence and Control of Time."

Now I'll share how the Law of Attraction relates to the 3 C's.

I summarize the 3 C's as

Charisma – They trust you

Confidence – You believe in you.

Control of Time – You get the most important things done; you do NOT procrastinate. And people trust this!

1. Charisma

I've talked with a number of people who say that they think charisma is something that one is "born with."

When talking with my college level, public speaking students, I note: "What we call charisma is often just referring to what I call *Magnetic Charisma*. Perhaps, the charisma of a young President Bill Clinton or Angelina Jolie. **There's more to charisma than that.**"

I go on to note:

Natural Charm Charisma: This is a form of charisma that comes easier to a person. For example, some people are not extroverts in their speech, but they're terrific listeners.

Warm Trust Charisma: This is the form of charisma that gains cooperation. People trust the charismatic person.

How Charisma Enhances the Law of Attraction in Your Life:

Specifically, with Warm Trust Charisma, people feel comfortable in your presence. You place them at ease. When they are comfortable and trusting, they're more likely to give you referrals and bring opportunities to you. It's not just who you know; it's about: *Do they trust you?*

You can enhance the Law of Attraction working in your favor with these trustworthy behaviors:

a) You fulfill your promises.

b) If something changes, you let people know quickly.

c) You avoid saying "yes" too much. (It's better to politely say 'no,' than to say 'yes' and later disappoint someone.)

d) You are a little early for all appointments.

e) You look out for the well-being of other people.

2. Confidence

In another part of this book, I speak of "ALF – adapt, learn, flex."

Here's the truth: Confidence is *not* about feeling comfortable.

I've given speeches with 723 people in the audience and networked at Stanford University and IBM. I was not fully comfortable during those times, but I believed in my rehearsal and preparation. I knew I could adapt and flex. Every speech has been a learning process for me, and each time I continue to improve because I adapt, learn and flex.

The confidence I possess is because of my diligent and intentional application of ALF (adapt, learn and flex) in every situation and challenge that presents itself in my life.

How Confidence Enhances the Law of Attraction in Your Life:

Simply put, confidence attracts. Why? All of us are aware of our own fears. It's great to be around someone who reassures us. Nelson Mandela later confessed that during the time he was in prison, he *was* afraid. But he did *not* reveal his fear to the other prisoners. In this way, the other prisoners were reassured.

So your confidence reassures others.

It's possible to feel some jitters in your gut, and still give a great speech. I've seen my clients and graduate students do that many times.

Get coaching and rehearse.

3. Control of Time

Let's face it: You'll do better when you attract people who *respect your time*. An old phrase is: "You teach people how to treat you."

Show people how you value time, and how you value *their* time. Arrive a bit early for appointments. Furthermore, do the most important things.

For example, my clients and I practice: "Worst first."

We identify the tough task (the "worst first") and do it *first*.

This practice drops much procrastination from your

life. People then trust you. And you're attractive for more opportunities.

Principle:
The Law of Attraction favors people who have worked to enhance their 3 C's: Charisma, Confidence and Control of Time.

Power Questions:
How can you practice more behaviors that inspire people to trust you?
How can you rehearse before tough events?
How can you focus your attention on "Worst first"?

When you're serious about unleashing the full potential of the Law of Attraction in your life, you'll take great care about focusing your thoughts and personal energy in a peaceful manner. Here are Jeanna Gabellini's insights about that process:

Peace is the Way
by Jeanna Gabellini

I've had several BIG aha moments in my life, **but the biggest transformation has come from a single focus ... peace.**
You'd think that with a business name like Master Peace Coaching my focus would always be about being at peace. Not so. I get caught in the same traps as everyone else when it comes to getting results, relationships and letting go of the past. I find myself focusing on single (not usually tragic) problems rather than being present to the

abundance right in front of my face.

This past week I was walking my daily route around the neighborhood and noticed a bright patch of green grass at the park behind my house. I stopped dead in my tracks and took a photo for you [on my blog].

Why?

Because for the past few months I've had internal conversations about the water drought in California causing the city to cut back on watering, which is killing the lawn at this normally lush park. I was bummed to see this beautiful spot go dry.

But that day my attention zeroed in on the one part of the lawn that looked really good. And I felt hope, appreciation, and abundance in that moment.

How often in your business do you zero in on all the areas that aren't working quickly enough? Or your mojo is crushed by that one person who didn't buy your offer, or walked out of your presentation? And have you ever made a sale but instead of celebrating you thought, "that's great but I need $XXXX more to make the bills?"

Here's my little trick to make a BIG transformation in your profits ... focus on peace. Make feeling at peace more important than making money, getting stuff done or getting it done right.

When I was at the worst period of my business (debt, no new clients and no new ideas to rescue it), nothing I did made a difference until I stopped trying so hard to make money. Being broke sucks, but the pressure I put on myself to turn it around was even worse. I felt helpless ... full of anxiety and judgment.

When I changed my focus to peace I felt empowered, in control and okay. When I wasn't focused on being broke I felt happy. I was living fully present to the resources and abundance around me. I still did the things I thought were good for my business, but I wasn't an emotional wreck in the process.

And that led to the business turnaround of the century. Nine months later I was debt free, making six-figures and feeling like I was walking my talk.

I had the same thing happen with a food addiction in my thirties. I had coaches, books and tools to break through the pain but nothing worked … until I made my focus peace instead of getting rid of my addiction.

Once you make friends with peace, all of the great tools that failed you in the past may be of huge value in your transformation because you are now present to let it in.

So, peace, baby! Peace. That's the most important thing (besides fun!).

Jeanna Gabellini is a Master Business Coach who supports conscious entrepreneurs to double (and even triple) their profits by leveraging attraction principles, proven strategies and fun. She is also the co-author *of Life Lessons for Mastering the Law of Attraction*, with Eva Gregory, Mark Victor Hansen & Jack Canfield. And her newest book: *10 Minute Money Makers: How to Easily Double Your Profits in Just 10 Minutes a Day!*

Combining vision, divine guidance and easy to implement actions, Jeanna delivers top-tier private coaching & sold-out seminars that have allowed committed entrepreneurs to blow past their self-imposed limits, ditch the drama of overwhelm and move into radical joy, inner peace and ever-increasing profits.

www.MasterPEACEcoaching.com

* * * * * *

Really leaping forward in life involves two things in

particular, the Law of Attraction *and* the Law of Creation. You might attract the best instruction and coaching, but if you do not take action and *create* with what you've learned, you'll remain stuck. Now Jeanna Gabellini provides key ideas about moving forward.

New Strategy Phobia
by Jeanna Gabellini

When I want something, I immediately go into action to get what I want. I don't do a bunch of research. I'm inspired and excited so I get my rear in gear.

This is not always the best way to be when choosing a new financial investment or choosing new strategies to build a business. I've been burned countless times because I didn't stop to ask myself how the strategy fit into my plan. I also never took the time to research what it would take to fully utilize the strategy for success.

Over time I became skeptical of trying new systems, strategies and technologies in my business. I didn't want to be that person who jumped on every new thing the experts promised would make me a million dollars ... and wind up broke and disappointed.

As usual, swinging from one side of a perspective to another doesn't solve your issues. I missed out on tons of awesome resources that my peers were using to uplevel their businesses. I made up a story that I wasn't smart enough to implement those same strategies in a way that got rockstar results.

After many years, I decided I'd had enough of "New Strategy Phobia."

Now when I hear a peer raving about something new

they are using to improve their business, I ask questions. I ask about the cost to implement it, the statistics, their overall strategy and what was involved to create a system around it.

Some people try all the latest 'whiz bang' strategies and talk about how amazing it is **BEFORE** they get results. In the past, I listened to those people because it was verrrry easy for me to jump on board based on their enthusiasm.

Other people test their strategies before they brag. Those are the people I listen to now. And then I still do some research, ask how it fits into my plan and implement with care and attention.

Another important question: Am I willing to do what it takes to keep the strategy or system working well?

During my last launch I installed a chat feature on one of my sales pages. Once installed, we planned for success. Who would man the chat line? How would I know if someone wanted to chat? Who would teach me how to use it?

My team and I created a system to handle this feature. My manager figured out how it worked and gave me a quick tutorial. We decided that I'd man the chat line when I was not on calls and she'd do it when I was busy. I made a Post-it note to remind me to turn on the system when I walked into my office each morning.

The chat feature was directly responsible for **over $10,000 in sales** during my launch. And it was fun chatting with the potential customers! The system to implement this new feature was critical for my success.

I also tried another new strategy during my launch that scared the pants off me ... Facebook ads! Several of my peers had been bragging about this for almost a year.

I immediately discounted it ...
- It'll cost too much money.
- I'd have to figure out the 'perfect' ad.
- How would I track the sales?
- That's for big-time marketers who have money to burn.
- Seems complicated. Too much to learn.

My friend, Justin, was getting phenomenal results with Facebook and he offered to teach me his formula. He does lots of testing before he shares his strategies. Guess what? **I made almost $5,000 of pure profit my first week using it, from people not previously on my email list! Happy dance!**

This is a strong nudge to try a new strategy in the next week. Do some research, make sure it's aligned with your plan and have some fun. May the results surprise and delight you!

Jeanna Gabellini is a Master Business Coach who supports conscious entrepreneurs to double (and even triple) their profits by leveraging attraction principles, proven strategies and fun. She is also the co-author of *Life Lessons for Mastering the Law of Attraction*, with Eva Gregory, Mark Victor Hansen & Jack Canfield. And her newest book: *10 Minute Money Makers: How to Easily Double Your Profits in Just 10 Minutes a Day!*

Combining vision, divine guidance and easy to implement actions, Jeanna delivers top-tier private coaching & sold-out seminars that have allowed committed entrepreneurs to blow past their self-imposed limits, ditch the drama of overwhelm and move into radical joy, inner peace and ever-increasing profits.

www.MasterPEACEcoaching.com

* * * * * *

A number of people lament that the Law of Attraction has not given them the big breakthrough. The truth is: there are certain elements that are holding the person back. I'm pleased to share with you Morgana Rae's insights in how you can break down internal barriers to the Big, Positive Transformation for your life.

How I Hit My FIRST 6-Figure Year
by Morgana Rae

Would you like to hear how I had my **FIRST 6-figure year?**

(And have been multiplying that ever since?)

This is a story I've shared with my coaching clients, but I don't think I've ever shared it publicly.

This happened nearly ten years ago. It really started with a shift of consciousness.

And then it got really messy. Totally not what I expected.

I had already slayed my money monster, and I had my Money Honey. My finances were stable. I was making a decent living, and I was aware that I was hitting a way-too-low ceiling of what was possible for me.

I made a decision, as I was designing my new lesson for the year, (those of you who have done the Renewal Ritual in my *Financial Alchemy* workbook on Amazon know what I'm talking about) that I was going to **"take off the limits of what I believed possible for myself."**

Boy did that change things for me! Because as soon as I took off the limits of what I believed possible for myself, **I took off the limits on what I'd been investing in my business.** I started spending money like someone who believed she was going to make 6-figures that year.

I bought all the classes, programs, and coaches I had been too cautious to buy in the past. I spent more than I ever had before. Without seeing my income rise.

It was like a bad joke. Not at all what I imagined when I set the intention to "remove limits."

By the time August came around, that year, **my bank account was at ZERO**. I swore to myself I wouldn't hire another coach.

But instead I charged another $8,000 to my credit card, transferred the balance to a 2.99% card, and flew across the country for a 2-day seminar on something I believed I needed to learn.

Because I believed in myself enough to invest with money I didn't have yet.

The teacher was awful. I don't recommend him. But someone IN the class with me made a suggestion* while we shared a cab ride back to the airport. I took her advice. And here's what happened:

I had my first $20,000 month when I got home.

Followed by my first $30,000 month.

Followed by my first $50,000 month.

I made over $100,000 in under 90 days! After never having reached that before in a 12 month period. **I was a bigger person, and I could never go back to playing small.**

I learned some golden lessons that still work for me today. Here are my **4 BIG TAKEAWAYS:**

1) If you want to succeed, you must make decisions from the perspective of your successful future-self.

Those decisions will always be more expansive and courageous than decisions based on fear and lack of confidence.

2) Don't let your circumstances make your decisions.

I invested in myself even when I had debt. Debt is temporary. Never wait until such-and-such happens to take action. That thing you're waiting for is waiting for YOU to step up. The clients and the money always come AFTER you act like the person you want to be.

3) My success doesn't depend on my coaches.

I'm going to get really honest and personal here. I've hired some truly terrible coaches. And I've made that "mistake" more than once. 'Cause I tend to see the best in everybody, and I assume other people share my values. So I paid tens of thousands of dollars for programs and promises they never delivered. Once I paid them I discovered I knew more than they did, made more money than they did, and had better relationships than they did.

I never asked for a refund. (I probably should have.) I always felt this is my business, so it's my responsibility to make sure I grow and get something I need from the experience.

Often the real value was the other people I met in the group.

Or it was seeing exactly what NOT to do in my own business.

Or simply the act of believing in myself enough to invest at such a high level.

And I always multiplied my income and my happiness anyway.

4) Be the kind of coach/service provider YOU would want to have.

When your competitors are under-delivering, maybe even bringing down your industry, **this is an *opportunity* to be the solution!** You may not see the rewards overnight, but if you keep plugging away, respecting yourself and your clients, and delivering superior service and results, it WILL catch up to you. And your success will last!

It ALWAYS comes down to finding opportunities, not excuses. No matter what.

The clients, the money, the relationships come AFTER you say yes to yourself.

Because that's how life works.

Namaste.

– Morgana Rae

* The whole time I was in the class, I was getting emails from clients who were having breakthroughs. In fact one of my clients hit his first million while I was at the seminar, and I read his email out loud to the class. The advice my seminar friend gave me was that, given my client results were so dramatic, I shouldn't charge less than $1,500. So I went home, raised my price from $375 to $1500, and immediately picked up 14 or 15 (It's so long ago I don't remember) new clients at the higher price. And 20 people hired me the next month. And so on. FYI… MORE people wanted to hire me as soon as I charged more.

Morgana Rae is an internationally acclaimed life coach, author, and professional speaker, and is regarded to be the world's top relationship with money coach. Morgana's groundbreaking program for attracting wealth has featured her in *Personal Excellence Magazine*, *Entrepreneur Magazine*, United Press International and The Wall Street Journal online. Morgana is the author of *Financial Alchemy: Twelve Months of Magic and Manifestation*, and she is a contributing author to the bestselling book *Inspiration to Realization*, ranked a "must read" by *Entrepreneur Magazine*. Morgana's *Financial Alchemy* books, CDs, magazine articles, and classes have impacted the lives of thousands of people worldwide. Morgana writes, speaks, and coaches from a desire to empower idealistic entrepreneurs, coaches, authors and artists to have a big impact in the world…and to heal the rift between heart, spirit, and money.

To Learn More Visit: www.abundanceandprosperity.com & www.morganaraemedia.com

BOOK TWO:
THE LAW OF ATTRACTION – ADDITIONAL TOPICS

For wealth creation and for manifesting loving relationships, the Law of Attraction forms a crucial component. In this section we'll cover these topics:

1) Get Unstuck! Use the Method: "Don't Replicate; Innovate"
2) Secrets You Can Use to Handle Fear and Really Succeed–and Enjoy Life!
3) Stay Strong and Get through Grief with Grace
4) Nonattachment and "Beware the Creeping Gray"

1) Get Unstuck! Use the Method: "Don't Replicate; Innovate"

Have you noticed that fear keeps us stuck? The Law of Attraction holds that if you spend too much time in fearful thoughts and feelings you will merely attract more fear!

At one point, I learned something *really important* about fear and getting unstuck.

To deal with fear, observe your first impressions, but do *not* stop there.

For example, one of my big fears is "wasted time." My time is full with work on my franchise *Jack AngelSword* and teaching graduate students and college students.

Now, imagine that you want to do something that can improve your career and that can help other people—But you do *not* feel you have the time.

That was my feeling in this particular situation: One of my focus areas is providing high-end coaching to a select clientele. The problem is (and here's where the fear of wasted time comes in): traditional sales techniques often involve a LOT of sales presentations that end in hearing the word "No." Unfortunately, such sales presentations that end in "no" feel like "wasted time" to me.

Further, attending networking events is often a go-to plan for someone selling a high-end service.

So this appears to be a conundrum. How can I be in two places at the same time? That is, how can I focus on my full schedule and still find new clients for my high-end coaching?

If I just focus on standard "sales techniques," I would just drop the whole idea of reaching new high-end coaching clients due to my lack of extra time.

Here's the solution:

Don't Replicate; Innovate.

After I observed my concern about "wasted time," I paused. Then I thought about DIFFERENT ways to introduce my high-end coaching to prospective clients.

Now, **my preferred way to gain a new coaching client includes this process:**

1. The prospective client sees my new 2 min. 40 second video. Instead of just a commercial; the video offers **valuable methods.** (Always make sure that the person gets value from interacting with you.)

2. The person calls my office. During the phone call, I pre-qualify the person by asking **three questions.**

3. I offer only five unique free coaching experiences per month—and such an experience is only available for qualified prospective clients.

All of the above conserves my time. The truth is: I take on few coaching clients. My service as a coach is in small supply.

Using a video saves a lot of time. For example, people can be watching the video while I'm asleep. (**During the video I provide a SOLUTION to a misconception about performing at your best during tough situations.** You can find this video on YouTube by typing "Tom Marcoux Reveals to Perform at Your Best".)

My point is: **You and I do NOT have to remain stuck in our fearful thoughts and impressions.**

We can do something new.

Yes, we'll need to step forth from our comfort zone.

We'll need to try new methods. Some of them will work and some will need to be refined. And likely, some experimental methods will need to be dropped.

I invite you to avoid dropping a new project just because your first impressions bring up fearful thoughts.

Remember: **Don't replicate; Innovate.**

2) Secrets You Can Use to Handle Fear and Really Succeed–and Enjoy Life!

Have you noticed that fear can stop you in your tracks? Fear can actually shutdown a positive pattern of thinking. The Law of Attraction reminds us to avoid letting ourselves stay stuck in fearful thoughts and fearful feelings. Otherwise, you'll attract more things in your life that inspire fear.

I'm really glad to share the following methods to help you

release yourself from fear.

First, we need to be aware that fear can shutdown our ability to think of options—and that can kill success You can observe that successful outcomes depend on *prior* successful thoughts and actions. I've learned a lot about handling fear as a feature film director, actor, guest instructor to MBA students at Stanford University, and entrepreneur in many tough and fear-inspiring situations. When you do anything that has high stakes, it helps to set successful patterns in *yourself* so you can perform at your best. We'll use the W.I.N. process:

W – will the power into Your Second Thought

I – increase flexibility (power of rehearsal)

N – nurture adaptability

1. Will the power into Your Second Thought

The verb *will* relates to "expressing determination, insistence, persistence."

We see this clearly when someone says, "I *will* walk for 30 minutes at lunchtime today."

Certainly that's more powerful than a wishy-washy phrase like: "I *hope* to walk for 30 minutes."

Let's look at how we can use the power of "I will" when it comes to handling fear.

Anytime you're going to do something for the first time, it's natural for fearful thoughts to arise. Someone may turn down a chance to give a speech because of the thought: "I'll choke up. I'll feel humiliated." Many people stop with this first fearful thought.

On the other hand, I now invite you to develop **The Power of Your Second Thought.**

In fact, it would be great for you to say, "I *will* develop the power of my Second Thought."

We may not be able to stop a first fearful thought from arising, but *we have the choice* to condition ourselves so that the *next thought* turns us toward an empowering direction.

Condition yourself to make Your Second Thought powerful.

How to Condition Yourself:

1) First, you need access to lots of empowering ideas. Read books, listen to audiobooks, attend workshops and see empowering videos. Learn from people who have accomplished what you want to do.

2) Write down and often review empowering ideas.

I take this another step further; I memorize empowering ideas. I memorize some phrases that I've written for my books including: "Keep score and achieve more." "Courage is easier when I'm prepared."

I also memorize other quotes written by others:

One can never consent to creep when one feels an impulse to soar. – Helen Keller

Here's an empowering phrase that I devised and an image to help my clients and college students become better public speakers: Picture a kind grandmother saying, "Feeling fear? Rehearse my dear."

I invite you to use this as your Powerful Second Thought. If you feel fear, remind yourself: "Feeling fear? Rehearse my dear."

2. Increase flexibility (power of rehearsal)

When you rehearse, you instill new patterns in your mind and in your body. When we first learn to do something, we feel awkward. After lots of rehearsal, we become good. We're even able to do some things well *unconsciously*.

I've studied acting, martial arts, public speaking, piano-playing, writing and more. All of this study and rehearsal has helped me perform at my best—even when I was scared.

For example, years ago, I arrived for a photo shoot for a top software company's website.

The photographer took one look at me and with a big frown said, "Oh. You were born in America." He had previously picked my headshot photo and had apparently wanted an Asian man born in an Asian country.

His reaction made me really afraid that I would be dismissed. I had spent funds on getting to the location and I did need to earn money that day.

Because of my training and rehearsal, my mind was flexible. I immediately said, "How about I put my hands like this. Like a Buddhist monk?"

I changed my posture from "brazen, shoulders thrown back, born-in-America guy" to humble, spiritual, calm guy.

"That will work," replied the photographer and he snapped a number of photos. He then paid me $400. That was the first time, I earned $400 in one hour.

For me that's the power of flexibility to help one in a scary situation.

3. Nurture adaptability

From years of rehearsing and giving speeches, I've developed my skills to answer spontaneous questions from the audience.

Effective action builds your confidence. You learn that you are flexible and that you adapt well.

Confidence is *not* about feeling comfortable.

It's about *knowing from experience* that you are flexible and that you adapt to various situations.

For example, I stood giving a speech to an audience at Sun Microsystems. One audience member asked, "What do you do when your boss does NOT listen to anything you say?"

For a moment, I was stumped. I was afraid.

But on the outside, *due to my rehearsals and developing my own techniques*, I said, "Julie, I can see that's important to you. I might need to pause for a moment. I want my comment to be useful for you."

By the time, I had finished saying this, my mind (working at about 700 words a minute*) found the answer: I said, "Quote your boss back to him. Then express what you want to say. Someone like your boss only cares about his own opinions and his own words. Fine. Say back his words to him. Then you'll have his attention, and then add your own idea."

[*Researchers suggest that human brains tend to operate at about 700 words a minute.]

So how do we deal with fear? We develop our own adaptability.

Another way to remember how to deal with fear is what I call *"ALF – Adapt, Learn, Flex."*

To create the joy, success and fulfillment you want, *rehearse and develop your skills to handle fear*. The bonus is: you simply enjoy more moments everyday!

> How will you nurture yourself and increase your adaptability?

---

3) Stay Strong and Get through Grief with Grace

Would you like to somehow stay strong even when you

are confronted with grief? The Law of Attraction invites us to flow into each present moment. Grieving is a natural part of life. And still, it helps to *not* get stuck. I've learned that I can feel grief for some moments off and on during the day — and still have some joy.

It is helpful to develop a healthy pattern when dealing with grief.

Yes, it can be a struggle to keep doing your job well enough and still give yourself the space to feel your feelings. Now, here's a process to help you stay strong and also "grieve with grace." For my clients, I have identified actions that can help you navigate your way through the grieving process. Here is the process:

C – contain
O – open to a Soothing Activity
M – move
F – focus through "good pace music"
O – offer helpful times and places
R – replace distractions
T – talk out feelings
S – support yourself (learning and some laughter)

1. Contain

My client Jerrie said, "I can't cry now. Once I start crying, I don't think I'll be able to stop. I work with some 'macho guys' and I'll look weak if I cry in front of them."

I replied, "Let me share a couple of ideas and you might find one or more of them to be helpful." At that point, I mentioned the value of having a "container for your grief." By this I meant: pick some time during the week to actually grieve. If you try to avoid all grieving, it can twist you up inside. Further, it may bubble up exactly at the wrong moment, such as when you're in front of people at work.

They could misinterpret your emotional outburst as an overreaction to something in the workplace (instead of your personal grieving).

Fortunately, my client Jerrie *set up a recurring Saturday therapy appointment* so she could cry out her feelings in a safe environment. After each therapy session, she took a walk to calm down. The physical activity also served as a transition before she continued with her day off.

2. Open to a Soothing Activity

By *Soothing Activity*, I mean an activity that gives you a break from your grief AND *fills your mind*. For example, I often work on a jigsaw puzzle while either listening to music or a stand-up comedian's routine. I find this to be a time to slow down and enjoy myself.

I mentioned "fill your mind." For some of us, meditation during grief is painful. Why? We slow down and our mind fills up with memories and painful thoughts. That's why I like to pick a Soothing Activity that engages my mind. For some, reading, singing or playing a musical instrument helps.

3. Move

Physical exercise can help you drain stress from your body. I often read and walk on a treadmill simultaneously. I find that reading takes my mind off the exercise and the time duration of the exercise routine.

4. Focus through "good pace music"

If you're concerned about focusing your mind for work, condition yourself to respond to "good pace music." By this I mean, some fast-paced music can speed up your efforts; for example, you can file paperwork at an efficient pace.

5. Offer helpful times and places

Using a timer can help you step into different "phases" during your day. If you're feeling sad, you might devote "the next 20 minutes to listening to sad songs." Then when the timer chimes, you can take a walk.

Sometimes grief robs us of energy. So you might use the timer to "focus for five minutes on paying bills." If there is a *set time with a limit*, we can often get ourselves to do an onerous task.

A place can serve as a trigger for certain feelings. Choose your triggers, that is, *choose a place with ca*re. If staying in the apartment you shared with a former partner brings you down, choose to step outside each day. Perhaps, take a walk at a nearby park or read a book at a local cafe. At some point, you might choose to move to another building or even another city.

If you need to get some work done, pick a particular chair and table to do your work. In essence, you condition yourself to get right to work when you're in a particular place.

My point is that you need to take extra care while you're grieving. You'll likely experience less energy so carefully arrange your schedule. Pick helpful times and places so you're able to function as you go through the necessary grieving journey.

6. Replace distractions

When you are grieving, you are likely in pain much of the day. So what do we do? We grab at any distraction available. Such a distraction robs us of time and can even put our job in jeopardy. Instead, consider working on a report by using your laptop (or mini-computer) with your Wi-Fi turned off. In this way, you'll have the chance to work on something without checking your email every couple of minutes. Be careful about distractions. It's reported that many people check their smartphones 150 times a day. Replace distractions and get the most important things done.

7. Talk out feelings

To whom can you turn and truly express your feelings? In the past, I've avoided burdening my friends with repeated heavy-emotional talks.

Instead, I've hired my own coaches and consultants for insight and times to talk about heavy issues.

If you're going through a truly tough time, consider hiring a therapist or counselor.

The truth is: If you can talk out your feelings, you'll press on through the grieving process. (I use the words "talk out" because it's helpful to get the feelings out into the open, to unburden your heart and to be able to "see them."]

On the other hand, if you don't talk out your feelings, you are likely postponing your pain and anger. Leaving pain and anger to fester can cause a serious disruption. Don't let that happen. *Find healthy ways to talk out your feelings.*

8. Support yourself (learning and some laughter)

Currently, I'm experiencing the process of supporting my mother in the last chapter of her life. This process is all new to me so *it's time for me to learn how to work with this situation.*

If you're going through a big grieving time, you might find a lot of support from reading books or listening to an audiobook. Let's face it. When something is tough and new to you, it really helps to hear how others endured and triumphed. To support myself, I purchased a highly recommended book by a gerontology expert who supported her mother in the last chapter of life. As you can see, I took action to find a resource in someone who had already dealt with this same tough situation.

Now, I'm adding a detail that may, at first, seem unusual. Consider finding chances for you to experience a bit of humor. I'm actually systematic about this. Every day, I see something funny on video at YouTube or via my digital video recorder (like TIVO). Why? Laughter releases endorphins and lowers one's stress levels.

I've noted that people experience moments of laughter even at funerals. These moments provide valuable relief!

How will you support yourself? And how will you gain more support from others?

_____

_____

4) Nonattachment and "Beware the Creeping Gray"

To really invoke the Law of Attraction in your life, it helps to practice nonattachment. Nonattachment includes holding preferences in your life but not staying stuck in "making demands."

For example, I may prefer that my friend Tami says kind things to me on a particular day, but I do not demand it. Perhaps, on a particular day, Tami is distraught over the ending of a romantic relationship. In her despair, she is abrupt with several people.

I am nonattached. I calmly view the situation as, "Tami is

in pain and she's doing the best she can."

If I were attached to insisting that Tami act "perfect," I might turn off the Law of Attraction. How? It would keep me in a rigid, upset state of mind.

Instead, I seek to flow with each moment.

I'll now share the process . . .

Uncomfortable in her hospital bed after neurosurgery, my mother started coughing. It felt like another insult to her injury . . . and a few hours later Robin Williams would gasp his last breath.

I'm mourning. My mother is in the last chapter of her life. This time is rough on her. Also today (8-11-14) Robin Williams ended his life. When an artist dies, I get sad about the ending of that artist's creativity. No more comedic lines to get us laughing. No more movie roles for the world to enjoy.

One thing that I have noticed is that each time I'm about to step into the hospital room where my mother lies so small and vulnerable, I feel dread. What's going to happen next? What am I going to see? Is she still going to be in restraints that stop her from pulling a feeding tube out of her nose?

So I start thinking in ways that create a low mood. I dread moments in advance. I dread calling my mother or talking with my father in anticipation of more bad news. This could be summarized as a fear of "what's next?"

However, I'm going to modify "What's next?" with something positive. I'll change it to *"What's next? — It might be good."*

This is my new *defiant stance*.

It's too easy to allow the dread of what bad things that *may* happen to color one's experience in the present moment. I call it *"The Creeping Gray."* (It bleeds *the life* out of us.)

Worry creates The Creeping Gray. Worry is NOT helpful.

A plan can be helpful. Action can be helpful. But anticipating pain before you step into the situation just ruins your present moment.

So I mention my defiant stance of "What's next?—It might be good." I've learned that we often *cannot* control the first thought that arises, but we can control what we do with it.

I'm interested in "The Power of the Second Thought."

In this situation, I turn around my first dread-filled thought of "what's next?" by *adding* **"It might be good."**

Things can become better and surprise you. For example, before my mother's surgery her hands and legs stopped working. She was bedridden. Now, after the neurosurgery her hands are stronger and she can lift her legs. So she might be on the road of recovering a lot of her ability to move. I hope so!

Some people are afraid to hope. They're afraid to have their hopes dashed.

Instead, I want to *avoid* living with no hope, just in the midst of "The Creeping Gray."

Now I invite you to observe yourself and your thoughts.
- Are you living a life of "gray"?
- Are you avoiding thoughts of hope because you are too afraid of having your hopes dashed?

Perhaps, you may want to adopt the phrase: ***"What's next?—It might be good."*** (Or it might be okay. Or it might be something that tests you and forces you to become deeper as a human being. It might make you more compassionate.)

You might find that you can lift your spirits up in this present moment if you adopt the defiant stance of "What's next?—It might be good."

Author Will Bowen emphasizes that life is meant to be challenging because "it keeps us engaged and growing."

I've learned that *I grow more by staying in the present*

moment.

If I jump ahead to worries about the future, I use mental discipline to bring myself back to the present moment.

The present moment is the only thing we truly have.

Stay present. Stay flexible. Experience good moments.

What would be good Second Thoughts that would help you?

_____

_____

BOOK THREE:
THE LAW OF CREATION –
ADDITIONAL TOPICS

For wealth creation and for manifesting loving relationships, the Law of Creation forms a crucial component. In this section we'll cover these topics:
 1) Release the Brakes: Use the 30-30-30 Shield
 2) Secrets So You Keep Going When You Feel "On Empty"

1) Release the Brakes: Use the 30-30-30 Shield

I've learned from working with 5,241 college students and graduate students that a number of people are slowed down by fear. Fear functions like a parking brake.

Do not keep it engaged. Instead, release the brake!

I've learned to use a method that I call *"The 30-30-30 Shield."*

Using this method began when I came across a particular quote:

When asked how she deals with a lot of pressure (as pro athlete, *Sports Illustrated* model, mother and wife of celebrity surfer Laird Hamilton), Gabrielle Reese said, "In life, you will always have 30 percent of the people who love you, 30 percent who hate you and 30 percent who couldn't care less."

We can use the above quote as part of what I call the "30-

30-30 Shield." How?

The ideas of Gabrielle's quote release us from trying to be perfect and from trying to please everyone.

Many of us experience a huge drop in energy and motivation when under-fire by others' criticism.

Your first thoughts might be on the order of: "Oh, no! I can't do anything right. Nobody's going to like my book, my blog, my artwork, etc."

Instead, invoke your 30-30-30 Shield.

You can assess: "Is this person part of the 30 percent who will never understand the value of what I'm doing? Are they someone who will never care? If so, *I can dismiss them* from my mind."

With the above, you could even "shield" your self-esteem. When someone slams criticism at us, it can feel like a blow to our self-esteem.

But with the 30-30-30 Shield we can assess: "This person just doesn't care about what I care about." or "Evidently, I made artwork that does not appeal to this person. I'll serve my own audience."

We can devote more time to thinking about the 30% who do love us:

Being deeply loved by someone gives you strength, while loving someone deeply gives you courage. – Lao Tzu.

In summary, guide your own thoughts. Don't let them fall into a negative spiral. Instead, employ your 30-30-30 Shield and rejoice in being fully alive. Experiment with creativity, take appropriate risks and concentrate on those people who can relate to your style of creativity. In this way, you have the Law of Creation functioning at full throttle in your life.

How will you move past fear? Will you change your perspective and let in the idea that it's likely that 30% of the people won't like what you're doing—and 30% won't care about what you're doing?

_____

_____

2) Secrets So You Keep Going When You Feel "On Empty"

"I can't keep going," my friend Trudy said, her eyes tearing up. "I've lost all the enthusiasm I had for writing my children's book. My inspiration's dried up. What was I thinking, anyway? This is just another project that I've started and stopped," Trudy continued.

Like many of us, Trudy stumbles and quits on her own project.

How about you? What new thing have you tried? Losing weight? Taking some classes? Have you had setbacks and have you given up?

Over the years, *I had to become an expert* about persisting and finishing projects.

Persistence turns out to be an important topic for my clients and college students. I'm not going to give you mere theories. As an author of 33 published books, I'll now share *Methods That Work*—not just theories. We'll help you be ONE of the few people who get big things done.

We'll use the O.N.E. process:

O – open to accountability

N – nurture breaks

E – enjoy progress (rewards and more)

1. Open to accountability

At the beginning of a project, it's often exciting. We're filled up with joy about possibilities. The creativity flows easily. Team members are excited.

Then there's a time in the middle of the project when it becomes "just work."

This is okay. If you know that you will endure a bumpy patch in the road, *you'll prepare for it!*

Patience, persistence and perspiration make an unbeatable combination for success. – Napoleon Hill

I encourage my clients and students to develop *"an Empowering Accountability."* By this I mean, you have a friend celebrate with you each step forward especially when it's hard. This can be as simple as leaving an email (for your friend) before you start a 20 minute session of writing. Then after you finish that 20 minute session, you send an email confirming that you kept your word and finished the writing session.

Your friend responds with something like: "Well done! Good work. You're getting closer to done. Good for you!"

A little more persistence, a little more effort, and what seemed hopeless failure may turn to glorious success. – Elbert Hubbard

Between goals and achievement are discipline and consistency.
– Denzel Washington

Set up your own schedule. Be accountable to yourself. Keep a Progress Log.

Get started. A paragraph each day. One drawing a day. A lot can be done with a little bit each day. One year of a drawing per day yields 365 drawings for an entire year. In this way, you energize the Law of Creation in your life.

2. Nurture breaks

Turning from the white board to my college students, I

said, "Take breaks or be broken." I then asked the illustration majors in the class, "Have you had an instructor suggest that you back away from your illustration and turn your head sideways or even turn the image upside down?"

Four students said, "No."

"No?!" I replied. "Then you're hearing one now."

I went on, "What do you get when you look at the image sideways?"

"A new perspective," two students replied.

Exactly. That is what a break can do for you! More than that, *a break can renew your energy* and even your feelings of hope.

Here Is Another Form of Taking a Break

Consider letting people know when you're on a roll and have momentum. In appropriate circumstances, you might say, "I'm in the middle of big deadlines. Please feel comfortable to contact me on ____ [10 days later.]"

I call the above practice a way of *"getting a break* from other people crashing down on your schedule."

If you're working on a personal project, you'll likely be considered odd (or even "obsessive") by family and friends.

Author Stephen King, at 67 says, "I still write everyday." He's completed and published 55 novels. That takes focus, effort and time.

Energy and persistence conquer all things. – Benjamin Franklin

Benjamin's idea may or may not apply, but I ask you: "How many people get something big done without energy and persistence?" . . . I rest my case.

Taking breaks provides a renewal of energy.

How can you take regular breaks?

3. Enjoy progress (rewards and more)

At this moment, I'm 53 days into one book project and I'm

37 days into another book project. Yes, I'm logging details because *I give myself credit* for my persistence.

I invite YOU to give *yourself* credit: Use a *Progress Log*.

And even reward yourself when you hit small milestones. Don't wait for anyone to reward you. You create your own mini-celebrations. It can be as simple as getting a cup of coffee or meeting with a friend.

At the end of our lives we all ask, "Did I live? Did I love? Did I matter?" – Brendon Burchard

The truth is: You are the one person who will most affect the course of your life. *You're the one* to come up with methods that work. Try some methods, use them and get new ones if they stop working for you.

I have no trouble dropping methods when they don't work, anymore. Why?

Because I think of life as a series of chapters.

Some methods work in your current daily routine. Then you move on to new techniques in the next chapter of life.

Never underestimate the power of the simple Progress Log to power up the Law of Creation in your life.

Glancing up I see my *5 Progress Logs* next to my computer monitor.

If you don't write 1,000 words a day, you're not serious about writing. – John Grisham

That works for John Grisham.

I suggest, if you're writing (or running), you can build up slowly.

It does not matter how slow you go as long as you do not stop.
– Confucius

Doing a big project is a marathon.

Take strategic breaks.

Be sure to "refuel your creativity tank." [Yes, I do retreat to a Disney Park every so often.]

See films, read books, do a puzzle, take a walk among trees, or anything else that helps you relax and feel an intrinsic joy.

Keep going.

How will you add appropriate breaks to your daily life?

_____

_____

BOOK FOUR:
THE LAW OF BEING – ADDITIONAL TOPICS

For wealth creation and for manifesting loving relationships, the Law of Being forms a crucial component. Sometimes, I view the Law of Being as "The Law of Renewal."

Additionally, the Law of Being includes ways for you to have a healthy, empowering mindset so you avoid losing personal energy. In this section we'll cover these topics:
1) How to Believe in Yourself When Others Don't
2) Improve Your Life and Relieve Yourself of Needless Suffering
3) Find Your OWN Path to Big Success and Lasting Happiness

1) How to Believe In Yourself When Others Don't!

Would you like to claim a gift that is uniquely yours? The gift is a nourishing belief when those around you fail to see your vision. We'll use the A.I.M. process:

A – acknowledge it's *your* destiny and not theirs
I – identify with your intuition
M – measure by your heart and NOT their approval

1. Acknowledge it's *your* destiny and not theirs

Here's a way you can *stay strong* even when you feel all alone and deeply disappointed that loved ones do *not* support you in *your* making your dream come true.

Perhaps, like many people, your loved ones are *afraid*. Maybe on a subconscious level they're afraid that you will get hurt as you step out of your comfort zone. Or even, *they feel uncomfortable* being around someone so focused and striving to fulfill his or her potential. Maybe they fear that you'll change and leave them behind when you do succeed on a significant scale. Sometimes we lose friends. Top author and speaker Larry Winget wrote: "Some friendships are like belts. We outgrow them."

Here's an important point to realize: *Other people cannot feel what you feel or intuitively know what you know.* Why? It is YOUR destiny—not their destiny. You're the one person who has all the clues and internal signs that your idea is a valuable one.

Perhaps, you've felt the gut-wrenching disappointment when a loved one does *not* support you in your pursuit of something that's close to your heart.

There is an answer to this. A neighbor of mine who races motorcycles competitively said, "In motorcycle racing, we're trained with the idea: *If in doubt, gas it out.*" The idea is to "pour on the gas." My neighbor assures me that if there's an irregularity in the road, more gas will help the motorcyclist get over the small ridge.

How can we apply *if in doubt, gas it out?* First, look to yourself for confirmation and energy. Add things that empower you. Often, when I'm writing I'm listening to empowering music. I read empowering books and I see uplifting films.

The point here is: You must take action to keep up your

own spirits.

2. Identify with your intuition

Above, I invited you to listen to yourself for confirmation.

Just because someone close to you cannot see or imagine your idea, it does NOT mean that they're right! It just means that they cannot feel the value of your idea.

Identify with your intuition and *not* their fears.

Many things that turn out well took time. For example, it took 8 years and many studios turning down the feature film *Splash* before it was produced, and Ron Howard directed the film. In fact, Disney turned it down the first time, and it was not until Disney *created a new division*, Touchstone Pictures, did *Splash* (starring Tom Hanks and Darryl Hannah) get made.

A truly famous example is how co-authors Mark Victor Hansen and Jack Canfield held to their intuition and endured 140 rejections before their book *Chicken Soup for the Soul* was published. The *Chicken Soup for the Soul* series has resulted in 250 additional titles and more than 500 million books sold.

Go by your intuition. Do not rely on others to "have all the answers." So-called experts can be wrong. You may be providing something that is new and different.

How can you recognize your "voice of intuition?"

Here's a quick description of two "voices."

- Voice of fear: contract, hide, do not experiment
- Voice of intuition: expand, build, take appropriate risks

Every day and really every moment, we have a choice. We can grow and expand and step toward our destiny. Or we can contract and hide and let doubters bring us down.

I invite you to *nurture yourself and step forward* into a steady pace to create something new and better in your life.

3. Measure by your heart and NOT their approval

In a way, I've been lucky that my father is stuck, for decades, in a disapproval mode. **I've learned to listen to my own heart and ignore his negativity.** The truth is he has had no experience related to being an entrepreneur, graduate school instructor, author, and feature film director. Sure, he has opinions—*uninformed opinions*.

I'm so glad that I ignored his narrow-viewed advice. My life has been so much more of a joyful adventure than merely playing it safe. His constant refrain is "survival." I've replied, "That's not enough. I want to thrive!"

Do you have someone close to you who simply does not support your vision?

Walt Disney's own wife, brother/business partner and board of directors were all against Disneyland. Why? There had never been a theme park before. In fact, Walt's wife Lillian asked Walt, "Why do you want to do an amusement park? They're so dirty." Walt replied, "Mine will be clean!"

Walt measured things by his own heart. In fact his first thoughts about creating an amusement park began in 1911 when as a child, he and his sister would stand outside the gates of a Kansas City amusement park. Finally in 1955, Walt opened *his own gates* of Disneyland. Can you hold on to an idea for 44 years? Will you take the steady steps necessary to move forward?

Novelist Greg Bear told me that it took 10 years for readers to discover one of his novels.

My point is that some dreams take several years—and several starts and stops and moments or months of discouragement.

Plenty of people, often those closest to us, will express their doubt. As emphasized in this section, it's really only natural because you are the one who hears your personal and unique "music."

Nurture yourself and your vision—energize the Law of Being in your life.

Get coaching and continue your efforts to learn more and more. [For more about coaching and to learn a powerful method to perform at your best when in a tough situation, see my video (just 2 min. 40 secs.) when you go to Youtube.com and type in the words "Tom Marcoux How to Perform at Your Best."

This world needs people who hold to their vision and persist.

Thank you!

Will you shift your focus from fear to your intuition? How will you make space in your life to listen to your intuition?

_____

_____

2) Improve Your Life and Release Needless Suffering

Would you like to move forward faster and shake off needless suffering? I've learned that often facing the truth may hurt in the short run but it eliminates a LOT of suffering. The Law of Being invites us to pay attention to releasing needless suffering.

We'll use the A.I.M. process:

A – arrange space to feel and assess the information

I – intensify your support

M – measure your new behaviors

1. Arrange space to feel and assess the information

A number of people keep themselves too busy to actually feel their feelings.

If you have a big decision to make, schedule some time. If possible, do make time to "sleep on it." You will likely have new thoughts and feelings upon waking up the next day.

Also assess the state of being in the person offering you advice.

Ask these questions in your own mind:
- Does this person really care about my well-being?
- Is this person operating out of fear?
- Is this person (even a family member) blinded by personal needs and fears? Does he or she have my well-being as central to his or her perceptions?

Often, what people say indicates THEIR story and not a focus on your journey.

Be careful.

Rest up.

Make space to refresh yourself so you can see more clearly.

2. Intensify your support

Facing the truth can be really painful and it may drain a lot of your energy. You might even fill up with fear.

The solution is to intensify the support you feel in your daily life.

My clients have . . .
- engaged a therapist
- joined a support group
- talked with a trusted family member or friend
- asked for help around the house in order to recover some personal energy

3. Measure your new behaviors

How do you know if you're really facing the truth? The answer is in your new actions. At one point, I saw that I was getting heavier than I preferred. How did I know that I was facing the truth? I logged my *increase* in daily exercise. I added more time on a treadmill and even raised the amount of weights I use in strength training.

The truth means a lot to me*.

*I even wrote a book entitled: *Truth No One Will Tell You: How to Feed Your Soul, Save a Business, or Get a Job During an Economic Crisis.*

* * *

Remember, when you face the truth, you can ultimately move forward faster and alleviate much needless suffering.

Use these methods:

A – arrange space to feel and assess the information

I – intensify your support

M – measure your new behaviors

Face the truth. Release yourself from needless suffering. Become stronger.

Your experience of life will improve!

What new behaviors will you measure?

_____

_____

_____

3) Find Your OWN Path to Big Success and Lasting Happiness

What do you rest your identity on? In other words: Who are you? And how do you feel about yourself?

As a feature film director, I've worked with classically attractive actors and models. Were they happy? Some of them. Others were on edge. You could see it in their eyes. It was as if their running monologue in their mind was: "If I'm not beautiful [handsome], what am I? Oh, hell! Another wrinkle! Another age spot!"

I invite you to *choose* the essence of your identity in ways that *empower* you. We'll use the O.N. process

O – organize your thoughts and beliefs

N – nullify the "seek approval trap"

1. Organize your thoughts and beliefs

Who do you think you are? What is good about you?

A number people define themselves by their roles: good parent, good spouse, good friend.

But there can be a problem here. What? How do you define any of the above roles? Do you define it by what *other* people say?

What if you make the right decision and curb the spending of your spouse, but your spouse gets angry? Some of us would feel bad. Some of us would even think: "If I was a better spouse, I'd make more money and I could get what my sweetie wants."

Really? Is that even true? Are more material things the solution?

I suggest you think of about three different elements as you consider the foundation for your identity: a) your values, b) "your being" and c) your actions.

Let's start with your actions. If you base your whole identity on what you do (say, your job), who are you when you're not doing that? By this, I mean let's avoid having your job be your complete identity. Why? Think about it. Who can a workaholic be if he loses his job? It's likely that he turns desperate and perhaps, depressed. With the job gone, his identity is gone.

So this observation leads us to also include two other elements for the foundation of our identity. *Let's focus on your values.* What is most important to you? I value being helpful to my graduate students/college students, my friends, my family, my clients and my readers. My personal mission is: "I help people experience enthusiasm, love and wisdom to fulfill big dreams." I value expressing my creativity.

Now it's your turn. Pull out a sheet of paper and write down what you value the most. Next, add "Things I do that support what I value." And note: "New actions I can take to support my values."

Finally, *let's talk about "your being."* Some years ago, my father said, "Do you duty." I replied, "I do my duty and it's not making me happy." The point here is that if you just aim to be a "human doing" instead of a human being, you most likely feel empty inside. How can that be?

A sense of well-being comes from more than mere achievements.

Imagine that "your being" comes from your "being present in this moment." It's not just about finishing some project and then you feel good. Take it from a guy who's directed feature films and published 33 books: Completing projects is enjoyable. However, I spend most of my time "in the process." So it's good to *stay in the present moment* and find meaning in this present moment.

You can be kind in this present moment. You can be creative. You can be loving. You can enjoy laughter. You can hug a loved one. *Be in this present moment.* (That's energizing the Law of Being.)

Also, schedule time to connect with that part of you that experiences calm and peace. For some of us, that's during prayer-time or quiet-time. Some of us only feel a few moments of comfort as we get into a hot bath. Whatever it is for you, connect with those moments. Engage those activities that allow calm and peace into your life. *Be* in the moment with them and the Law of Being will in turn *bless your life.*

2. Nullify the "seek approval trap"

Some of us set up our identity based on someone's approval. It's a trap!

Why? Some people will never give you approval. It helps to let that go. One of my friends is a snob, and he had disparaging words for one of my books. Fine. I did NOT write that book for him. I let his words go. I'm not seeking his approval.

The secret of leadership is simple: Do what you believe in. Paint a picture of the future. Go there. People will follow. – Seth Godin (in his book Tribes*)*

Many people can tell you about how "no matter what I try, my parent never thinks I'm good enough."

For example, my client "Ellie" endures the burden of dealing with her bitter, judgmental mother.

"You're wrong!" her mother yelled.

Ellie found her voice and replied, "No. I'm different." Ellie learned to find other people who appreciated her as she is. She also learned to value herself on her own terms.

Instead of putting the control of your life into *someone else's hands*, consider making your own choices. Identify your own personal standards.

Don't merely concentrate on getting your preferred results. I've learned that hoping for "perfect audience reactions" can be quite disappointing. Take action and find your meaning in the action. You want to be a kind person—act in kind ways. You want to be a courageous person—take appropriate risks.

Today, I read parts of a book I wrote back in 1989. Ouch. I write better today. And I celebrate that! I celebrate that I had the courage to write my first book back in 1989.

I celebrate that I've written more than 1 million words. I have improved in my craft over the years.

So drop the "need for approval trap." Practice *your* craft. Learn as you go.

Here's how you find your OWN path for big success and lasting happiness: **Develop your OWN criteria for your identity. Drop seeking approval to validate yourself.**

Instead, empower your own foundation of your identity. Choose your values well, choose "your being," and choose your actions.

From whom do you seek approval? How can you shift to a quiet sense of earning your own approval and appreciation?

_____

_____

A FINAL WORD AND SPRINGBOARD TO YOUR DREAMS

Congratulations on your efforts as your worked with the material in this book. To get even more value from this book, take the plans and insights that you created and place them in some form in your calendar or day planner. *Plan and take action.* Return to these pages again and again to reconnect with the material and take your life to higher levels.

The best to you,
Tom

Tom Marcoux
Executive Coach - Spoken Word Strategist

Special Offer Just for Readers of this Book:

Contact Tom Marcoux at tomsupercoach@gmail.com for special discounts on **coaching,** books, workshops and presentations. Just mention your experience with this book.

==> See an Excerpt from Tom Marcoux's book, *Darkest Secrets of Persuasion and Seduction Masters: How to Protect Yourself and Turn the Power to Good* – on the next page.

Excerpt from
Darkest Secrets of Persuasion and Seduction Masters: How to Protect Yourself and Turn the Power to Good
by Tom Marcoux, Executive Coach – Spoken Word Strategist
Copyright Tom Marcoux

... Now, I am in my 40's, with gray in my hair, and for 27 years I have been taking action to protect people.

And now is the time for me to protect you with the Countermeasures I reveal in this book.

Every human being needs to be able to break the trance that a Manipulator creates.

You need to make good decisions so you are safe and you keep growing—and you are not cut down and crippled.

This Darkest Secrets material is so intense that I first released it only with the counterbalance of my most energizing and uplifting books, *Nothing Can Stop You This Year!* and *10 Seconds to Wealth: Master the Moment Using Your Divine Gifts.*

An interviewer asked me: "Who can be the Manipulator?"

A co-worker, a boss, a salesperson, someone you're dating, and someone you think is a friend.

Now is the time—this very minute—for me to write this book to protect you.

I must speak the truth.

These Darkest Secrets of "persuasion masters" are ...

Wait a minute! Let's say it plainly: These are the Darkest Secrets of masters of manipulation. Throughout this book, I will call these people what they are: Manipulators.

Dictionary.com defines "manipulate" as "To influence or manage shrewdly or deviously.... To tamper with or falsify for personal gain."

In this book, we will look on a manipulator as one who deviously influences someone with no concern about that person's well-being, and who causes harm to that person.

Here is the first Darkest Secret:

Darkest Secret #1:
Manipulators Make You Hurt
and Then Offer the Salve.

Manipulators would invite you to go out in the sun for hours and then sell you the salve to soothe your burns. The problem is that we don't notice that this is what they're doing.

For example, you're considering the purchase of a house. A Manipulator asks the question, "So, where would you put your TV?" This question is designed to put you into a trance.

Dictionary.com defines "trance" as "a half-conscious state, seemingly between sleeping and waking, in which ability to function voluntarily may be suspended." Let's condense this: in a trance you may not be able to function freely.

Here is the second Secret:

Darkest Secret #2:
Manipulators Put You into a Trance.

To protect yourself, you must learn to use Countermeasures to Break the Trance.

All the Countermeasures (actions you can take to break the trance) in this book will make you stronger and more capable of protecting yourself.

Now, we'll view the third Secret:

Darkest Secret #3:
Manipulators Care Nothing for You and Human Decency: They'll lie, cheat, and do whatever they need to do so they win—but their charm masks all this.

Let's return to the example of a Manipulator selling you a house. A Manipulator does not pause for an instant to see if you can truly afford the new house. The Manipulator would neglect to mention that you will not only have your mortgage payment of $900. There will be additional costs: home repairs, property tax, water, electricity, homeowner's insurance, and more. The Manipulator only emphasizes what he or she knows you want to hear: "Look! $900 is better than the $1500 you're paying for rent, which is just going down the toilet. And the $900 is an investment."

Let's go back to **Darkest Secret #1:**
Manipulators make you hurt and then offer the salve.

The Manipulator has you feeling good about the solution (salve) and feeling bad about your current life situation.

How? A Manipulator will make you hurt through questions such as:

- What bothers you about paying $1500 a month for rent?

(The Manipulator will use a derisive tone when he says the word *rent*.)
- What is *not* smart about paying rent on someone else's house instead of investing in your own house?
- How do you feel about your children walking in the neighborhood where you live now?

Do you see how these questions are designed to make you hurt enough so that you'll buy?

An interviewer asked me, "Tom, aren't these good arguments for purchasing a house?"

"What we're looking at is the *intention* of the influencer," I replied. "Let's look at our definition of a manipulator as one who deviously influences someone with no concern about that person's well-being, and who causes harm to that person. If the person truly cannot afford the house, he or she will be harmed by buying it. If the manipulator conceals the truth, the manipulator is doing harm. That's the important difference."

Some friends of mine are ethical and helpful real estate agents who truthfully reveal the whole situation and help the purchaser achieve her own goals.

In this book, we are talking about another type of person; that is, unethical Manipulators.

* * *

In any given moment, we need to remember the tactics Manipulators use. We will focus on the word D.A.R.K. so you can remember details easily and protect yourself from Manipulators.

D — Dangle something for nothing
A — Alert to scarcity
R — Reveal the Desperate Hot Button
K — Keep on pushing buttons

1. Dangle Something for Nothing

What do conmen and conwomen do to seize your attention? They make you think you're getting a "steal."

I recently saw a documentary in which a conman on a street in England showed a toy that looked like it was dancing. This fake product was actually dancing because of a hidden, invisible thread. The conman was dangling something for nothing. The Entranced Buyer thought he was getting something worth $20 for only $5. That was the trick. The Entranced Buyer felt that he was getting $15 extra of value for his $5. What the Buyer really got was something worth nothing. Similarly, I know someone who purchased a copy of a Disney movie from a street vendor in San Francisco. She brought the copy home and it was unwatchable—and the street vendor was never seen again.

An old phrase goes, "A conman cannot con someone who is not looking for something for nothing."

How to Protect Yourself from "Dangle Something for Nothing"

Stop! Get on your cell phone and talk through the "deal" with someone you know who thinks clearly. Go home. Think about it. Do some research on the Internet. Listen to your gut feelings. If the salesman or conman is too insistent, get away from that Manipulator. Get quiet. Have a cup of water. Cool down. Break the Trance!

Break the Trance and Identify the Crucial Detail

Earlier, I mentioned that a Manipulator puts you into a trance. An added problem is that we put ourselves into a trance. For example, as you read this, are you thinking about your right toe? Most likely not (unless you stubbed your toe recently). The point is that we only focus on a tiny percentage of what is going on in our life.

Around fifteen years ago, I caused myself trouble because I put myself into a trance. I discovered that under certain conditions, friendship can make you nearly deaf. Here's how: I was producing a song for a motion picture. A good friend was singing backup in the chorus. Because of our friendship, I wanted him to sound great. I completely missed the Crucial Detail. In this kind of situation, the Crucial Detail is that what truly counts is how the lead singer sounds! I made a song that I could not release. What a waste of time and money! I had put myself into a trance.

In any situation in which the Manipulator is "dangling something for nothing," we often fall into a trance and miss the Crucial Detail. The most important detail is *not* that we're saving money if we order before midnight tonight. What counts is whether the product creates a lasting, crucial benefit in our lives. And is the benefit of the product worth the cost? Some people even program themselves to make mistakes by saying, "I can't pass up a bargain." The bargain is *not* the Crucial Detail.

Secrets to Break the Trance

This is the process of B.R.E.A.K.S. It will help you remember the proven methods to break a trance.

B — Breathe
R — Relax
E — Envision
A — Act on aromas
K — Keep moving
S — Smile

Secret #1: Breathe

Remember Secret #1: Manipulators make you hurt and then offer the salve. The Manipulator wants to put you into a state of being that fills you with a sense of urgency and anxiety. Oh, no! I'm going to miss the sale!

Stop this highly vulnerable state. Take a deep breath. Do it now. Take a deep breath and let your belly "get fat" by filling it with air. As you breathe out, let your belly deflate. Breathe in through your nose and breathe out through your mouth. This is called belly-breathing. Repeat the actions of belly-breathing three times. Good. Now, do you feel different? Remember, when you are relaxed, you are strong.

Secret #2: Relax

You become stronger when you condition yourself to relax in the face of adversity. Researchers note that when an Olympic athlete is confronted with the most stressful moment in her life, she has prepared in advance. She has given herself ways to calm down. Two powerful methods are described in this section about B.R.E.A.K.S. One is breathing, and the other is envisioning.

A special part of relaxing is the effective use of your posture. Many of us think that we're relaxed when we slouch. However, I was taught by three physical therapists that when you sit up and align your vertebrae, you are more relaxed because your back's bone structure is naturally supporting you. Many of us discover that placing a pillow behind the lumbar-area of our back helps us sit up better. If you are sitting or standing when talking with a Manipulator, ensure that your posture is aligned. You will have more power to protect yourself.

Secret #3: Envision

Envision an image that makes you feel strong. Often, our strongest images come from movies that we saw when we were young. Some of my clients envision being strong like Xena the Warrior Princess or Superman. One client thinks of Sean Connery as James Bond. Immediately, this client walks smoothly with poise. He feels confident. Act as if you are, and you are!

Also, envision yourself being quite aware of your surroundings. On vacation, many of us become entranced by our new surroundings. Travelers let their guard down. A conperson catches them at a weak moment. It's important to stay in the present and be alert to what's going on. Stay present with your needs, and shop around before making a large purchase. Be prepared to walk away.

Watch out for Manipulators who are slick, fast talkers. They try to get your money, and just minutes after they succeed, you realize what happened.

But this is *not* for you! You can remind yourself with an internal comment: "I am aware. What is really going on here?"

Secret #4: Act on Aromas

Let's notice the power of an aroma.

Smell is a potent wizard that transports you across thousands of miles and all the years you have lived. – Helen Keller

Nothing is more memorable than a smell. One scent can be unexpected, momentary and fleeting, yet conjure up a childhood summer beside a lake in the mountains. – Diane Ackerman

You need to be able to calm down within seconds. One of the fastest ways to do that is to use a favorite aroma. One of my clients has conditioned herself to calm down by smelling lavender. The process for her was to recline in a hot bath and smell lavender simultaneously. Now, the smell of lavender relaxes her limbs quickly.

Remember, when you are relaxed, you neutralize the Manipulator's tactic to make you feel that buying something now is an urgent matter. You let go of any anxious feelings the Manipulator seeks to create in you. Use an aroma to help you feel relaxed and strong.

Secret #5: Keep Moving

A trance often transfixes or freezes us, making us still. Sometimes, the most powerful way to break a trance is to use a movement that you prepared in advance. One of my clients closes his right fist and taps it on his right thigh. In his mind, he repeats the phrase: "I am my own person!" This helps him break out of a trance induced by a Manipulator.

Another client quietly snaps her fingers near her waist. This reminds her to "snap out of it."

Excerpt from
Darkest Secrets of Persuasion and Seduction Masters: How to Protect Yourself and Turn the Power to Good

Purchase your copy of this book (paperback or ebook) at Amazon.com or BarnesandNoble.com
See **Free Chapters** of Tom Marcoux's 33 books at http://amzn.to/ZiCTRj

ABOUT THE AUTHOR

You want more and better, right? Imagine fulfilling your Big Dream.

Tom Marcoux can help you—in that he's coached thousands of people: CEOs, small business leaders, graduate students (at Stanford University) speakers, and authors.

Marcoux is known as an effective **Executive Coach** and **Spoken Word Strategist.**

(and Thought Leader—okay, writing 33 books helped with that!)

** *CEOs, Vice-Presidents, Other Executives, Small Business Leaders:*

You know that leading people and speaking at your best can be tough.

Marcoux solves problems while helping you amplify your own Charisma, Confidence and Control of Time.

Interested? Email Marcoux—tomsupercoach@gmail.com

Ask for a *Special Report:*

* 9 Deadly Mistakes to Avoid for Your Next Speech

** *Speakers, Experts—for a great TED Talk, Book, Audio Book, Speeches, YouTube Videos.*

Marcoux solves problems while helping you to make your Concise, Compelling Message that gets people to trust you and get what you're offering (product, service, *an idea*).

Yes—the *San Francisco Examiner* designated Tom Marcoux as "The Personal Branding Instructor." Marcoux is a professional member of the National Speakers Association for 15 years.

Marcoux is an expert on STORY. He won a Special Award

at the EMMY AWARDS, and he directed a feature film that went to the CANNES FILM MARKET and earned international distribution.

(Marcoux helps you *Be Heard and Be Trusted* . . . that's his 15th Anniversary, 3rd edition book.)

As a CEO, Marcoux leads teams in the United Kingdom, India and the USA. Marcoux guides clients & audiences (IBM, Sun Microsystems, etc.) in leadership, team-building, power time management and branding. See Tom's Popular BLOG: www.TomSuperCoach.com

Specialties: coach to CEOS * Executives * Small Business Owners * Leaders * Speakers * Experts * Authors * Academics

One of his *Darkest Secrets* books rose to #1 on Amazon.com Hot New Releases in Business Life (and in Business Communication). Marcoux is a Executive Coach and guest expert on TV, radio, and print.

Marcoux addressed the National Association of Broadcasters' Conference six years running. With a degree in psychology, Tom is a guest lecturer at **Stanford University**, DeAnza College & California State University, and teaches business communication, designing careers, public speaking, science fiction cinema/literature and comparative religion at Academy of Art University. He is engaged in book/film projects *Crystal Pegasus* (children's) and *Jack AngelSword* (thriller-fantasy). See Tom's well-received blogs

at www.BeHeardandBeTrusted.com

at www.YourBodySoulandProsperity.com

Consider engaging **Tom Marcoux as your Executive Coach.**

"As Tom's client for many years, I have benefited from his wisdom and strategic approach. Do your career and personal life a big favor and get his books and engage him as **your Executive Coach."** – Dr. JoAnn Dahlkoetter, author of *Your Performing Edge* and Coach to CEOs and Olympic Gold Medalists

"Tom Marcoux coached me to get more done in 10 days than other coaches in 2 years." – Brad Carlson, CEO of MindStrong LLC

Tom Marcoux can help you with **speech writing** and **coaching for your best performance.**
As Tom says, *Make Your Speech a Pleasant Beach.*
Join Tom's Linkedin.com group: *Executive Public Speaking and Communication Power.*
At Google+: join the community "Create Your Best Life – Charisma & Confidence"
Get a **Free** report: "9 Deadly Mistakes to Avoid for Your Next Speech and 9 Surefire Methods" at
http://tomsupercoach.com/freereport9Mistakes4Speech.html

Tom Marcoux has trained CEOs, small business owners, and graduate students to speak with impact and gain audiences' tremendous approval and cooperation. *Learn how to present and get thunderous applause!*
"Tom, Thanks for your coaching and work with me on revising my speech at a major university. Working with you has been so enlightening for me. Through your gentle prodding and guidance I was able to write a speech that connects with the audience. I wish everyone could experience the transformation I have undergone. You have helped me discover the warm and compelling stories that now make my speech reach hearts and uplift minds. This was truly an empowering experience. I cannot thank you enough for your great assistance." — J.S.

"Tom Marcoux has been an NAB Conference favorite [speaker] for six years. And he is very energetic."
– John Marino, Vice President, National Association of Broadcasters, Washington, D.C.

"Using just one of Tom Marcoux's methods, I got more done in 2 weeks than in 6 months."
– Jaclyn Freitas, M.A.

Tom's Coaching features innovations:
- Dynamic Rehearsal
- Power Rehearsal for Crisis
- The Charisma Advantage that Saves You Time

Become a fan of Tom's graphic novels/feature films:
- Fantasy Thriller: *Jack AngelSword*
  type "JackAngelSword" at Facebook.com
- Science fiction: *TimePulse*
  www.facebook.com/timepulsegraphicnovel
- Children's Fantasy: *Crystal Pegasus*
  www.facebook.com/crystalpegasusandrose
- Young Adult Fantasy: *Jenalee Storm*
  At Facebook.com "Jenalee Storm."

See **Free Chapters** of Tom Marcoux's 33 books at http://amzn.to/ZiCTRj   Amazon.com

Your Notes:

_____

_____

_____

www.ingramcontent.com/pod-product-compliance
Lightning Source LLC
Chambersburg PA
CBHW070456100426
42743CB00010B/1648